CALLED TO BE
HOLY

Growing in the Likeness of Jesus

RICHARD R. MELICK JR.

LifeWay Press®
Nashville, Tennessee

ISBN 978-1-4300-3195-6
Item 005644106

Dewey decimal classification: 234.8
Subject heading: SANCTIFICATION

To order additional copies of this resource, write to LifeWay Church Resources Customer Service; One LifeWay Plaza; Nashville, TN 37234-0113; fax 615.251.5933; phone toll free 800.458.2772; email *orderentry@lifeway.com;* order online at *www.lifeway.com;* or visit the LifeWay Christian Store serving you.

Printed in the United States of America

Adult Ministry Publishing
LifeWay Church Resources
One LifeWay Plaza
Nashville, TN 37234-0152

To my wife, Shera,
and my children,
Rick and Joy Melick, Kristi and Michael Ent,
and Karen and Darren Draeger,
who share the quest for holiness,
and to my grandchildren,
Richard and Nathan Melick;
Anna, Michael David, Abigail, and Samuel Ent;
and Rachael and Madeline Draeger,
whose young hearts are already sensitive to the Lord.

THE AUTHOR

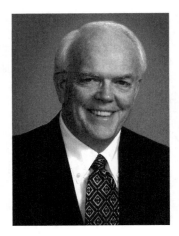

Dr. Richard R. Melick Jr. serves as director of the academic graduate-studies program (ThM and PhD) and as distinguished professor of New Testament studies at Golden Gate Baptist Theological Seminary. He has been at Golden Gate since 1996. Prior to that, he was the president of the Criswell Center for Biblical Studies in Dallas. Dr. Melick has served at six other educational institutions during his teaching ministry, as a professor, an academic vice-president, and other administrative positions. Since 1986 he has also been a professor at the Evangelische Theologische Faculteit in Heverlee, Belgium.

A former pastor of two churches and numerous interim pastorates, Dr. Melick is a recognized author. He serves as a consulting editor for the *The New American Commentary* and wrote the series' first volume on Philippians, Colossians, and Philemon. He also served as a coeditor and contributor to *Authority and Interpretation: A Baptist Perspective*. He coauthored with his wife, Shera, *Teaching That Transforms: Facilitating Life Change Through Adult Bible Teaching* and has contributed to many other volumes. He was a translator of the Holman Christian Standard Bible and authored some of the notes in the Study Bible edition and the Apologetics Study Bible edition.

Dr. Melick has three children, all in Christian ministry, and eight grandchildren. His hobbies include golf and motorcycling.

CONTENTS

PREFACE

Called to Be Holy surveys an important biblical theme. Holiness begins with God Himself—the model for all holiness. God's holiness never changes; it undergirds all of life for believers and unbelievers alike. Christians are called to be like God—to be holy. We learn what holiness means by focusing on Jesus Christ. He became flesh, in part, to show us how to live as we ought.

Holiness doesn't just happen in a believer's life. No one can be holy without God's grace. Paul said:

> The grace of God has appeared with salvation for all people,
> instructing us to deny godlessness and worldly lusts and to
> live in a sensible, righteous, and godly way in the present age,
> while we wait for the blessed hope and appearing of the glory
> of our great God and Savior, Jesus Christ. He gave Himself for
> us to redeem us from all lawlessness and to cleanse for Himself
> a people for His own possession, eager to do good works.
>
> **TITUS 2:11-14**

God's grace enables Him to forgive our past, and His grace mysteriously enables us to overcome sin in our Christian lives. In relating to us by grace, He changes us into the holy character that He desires.

Christians must continually determine how best to represent Christ. Our lives stand as lights to a dark world, pointing people to God's standard, which is the measure of the stature of Jesus Christ (see Eph. 4:13). The world influences us so much that we have great difficulty keeping our spiritual equilibrium. So unfortunately, the church sometimes looks more like the world than the world does.

The study has a twofold purpose:

1. To present the doctrine of holiness in a readable, understandable way

2. To encourage Christians to pursue holiness personally

I've tried to organize the book in a useful, readable way. The text offers simple but important steps for attaining holiness. I haven't unnecessarily included Greek and Hebrew words and technical exegesis. However, I've included many Scripture references to support the points. Chapters are divided into sections that provide a framework for understanding personal transformation. Because holiness is about transformation, I pray the book will challenge each reader's life as well as enlarge the mind.

I'm grateful to those who supported me in writing this study. Don Atkinson, an experienced editor, graciously invited me to write and provided expert help in producing the original 2001 edition. Kristi Ent, my daughter, offered valuable suggestions as well as loving support. Jeff Iorg, the president of Golden Gate Baptist Theological Seminary, always encourages me in my writing and other ministry. I appreciate his friendship and continuing support. My colleagues at Golden Gate constantly befriend, encourage, enrich, and challenge me to pursue the things of God and His kingdom. I'd also like to thank Sam House, Chris Johnson, David Haney, and Elizabeth Hyndman, who prepared the book for its 2014 rerelease.

I'm indebted to what I have learned from my family through the years. Shera, my wife, has lived in such a way that I'm constantly challenged by her holy character, enriched by her companionship, and encouraged by her constant love. My three children and their spouses—Rick and Joy, Kristi and Michael, and Karen and Darren—have enriched my life by their lives, their love for our Lord, and their faithfulness in responding to God's call for them to enter the ministry. Watching them, I have seen holiness displayed in the uniqueness of wonderful individuality. Finally, my eight young grandchildren—Richard, Nathan, Anna, Michael David, Abigail, Rachael, and Madeline—constantly remind me of the good things of life and challenge me to better living with their profound but simple faith in Christ.

During the writing process I've had two constant prayers. With an increasing longing to be more like Jesus Christ, I've prayed that in some way I too will display His holy character. I've also prayed that the truths here will encourage others to be like Jesus Christ as well. In short, my hope is what I've constantly prayed for 35 years—the same thing the apostle Paul prayed for the church at Philippi:

> This is my prayer: that your love may abound more and more in knowledge and depth of insight, so that you may be able to discern what is best and may be pure and blameless until the day of Christ, filled with the fruit of righteousness that comes through Jesus Christ—to the glory and praise of God.
>
> **PHILIPPIANS 1:9-11**

CHAPTER 1

HOLINESS—GOOD FOR ALL OF US

Holiness, holiness, is what I long for.
Holiness is what I need.
Holiness, holiness
Is what You want from me.[1]

The catchy tune and simple song grab our attention, and we easily join in the musical prayer. The song should express everyone's desire. All believers should long for holiness, righteousness, and faithfulness. If we really long for holiness, we've changed from self-centeredness to a desire for God's will. Nothing more accurately describes the life of a Christian than the desire to be holy.

ATTITUDES TOWARD HOLINESS

Holiness has seldom been popular. Being holy means people accept a different lifestyle from the norms of society. Many think of holy people as bizarre and eccentric. They consider holiness as something reserved for a select few who are called to be holy men, shamans, prophets, or priests. Through the centuries many have hoped others would be holy for them, assuming God has called priests, monks, nuns, and preachers to be holy.

What images come to mind when you think of the word holy?

What do you think is required for a person to be holy?

The average person seems to have trouble keeping up with the demands of life, and taking on the burden of holiness only adds to the frustration. Increasingly, society considers religious people as its major problem rather than the solution to its ills. After all, most religions stand against many accepted social values such as following passions and pursuing wealth and pleasure as the ultimate goal. For many, holiness applies to those whose dress is out-of-date, who refuse to enjoy modern entertainment, and who decry others who want to have fun in life.

These anti-Christian attitudes have been encouraged by two trends.

1. INCREASED SECULARISM. Church attendance has decreased, and most religions report fewer followers. The media encourage pleasure and ego satisfaction as the highest good. They entice people away from theistic roots and traditional values. Secularism focuses on the immediate and erodes the commitments of the most devout.

2. THE CONFUSION OF GOOD AND EVIL. The rise of witchcraft, Satanism, naturalistic religions, New Age beliefs, and atheism undermines Christian faith. It's common today to hear people advocate sexual promiscuity, extramarital affairs, unethical behavior, and deceit. Individuals and groups directly attack God and His Word. The undertow of modern life pulls all of us toward the sea of relativism.

How have you observed the decline of a holy lifestyle in our society?

How has the church responded?

Generations of Christians have fought battles against the inroads of secularism. Since the early 1900s many church leaders have preached the need for Christians to live separate lives. The most extreme separatists decried the ills of almost everything their contemporaries embraced. It was normal to hear admonitions against the evils of dancing, drinking, movies, pool halls, rock music, and so on. Many preachers said genuine Christians shouldn't associate with people who didn't live according to these convictions.

Separatists had high ideals, but they often reduced Christian holiness to lists of do's and don'ts. Many issues on their lists couldn't be found in the Bible, but lists provided clear-cut answers to the questions of godliness. The problem is that although these people had legitimate concerns, they often misunderstood true biblical motivations for godliness. Many of them also misapplied Scripture to situations it never intended to address. At conversion God delivers us from the Old Testament laws and regulations. He doesn't expect Christians to trade the Old Testament law for another "Christian law" to measure our spiritual successes. God desires a more dynamic relationship with His people.

The separationists had a basically negative view of the world. While acknowledging the world as God's handiwork, they also saw it as the home of Satan and evil. For many, culture was incurably evil. The only way to develop holiness was to flee culture. God's way was always different from the world's, and to be a Christian meant to be different.

How have you seen Christians try to impose laws of holiness on others?

What was the result?

This approach to Christian living brought strong reactions. The Baby Boomer generation asked serious questions about virtually everything. In the 1960s and '70s rebellion was in the air. People rebelled against established government; religion; social mores; family; and most of all, rules. Christians also asked questions. Why were the do's and don'ts advocated by past generations so binding? Does God really expect His people to be horribly out of step with society, as so many had advocated? Was there any real virtue in being "odd for God"? That type of "holiness" often repelled non-Christians. Hardly anything would attract them to the faith as long as *separation* was the watchword.

Some of the most effective communicators of the gospel changed the tone of their preaching to a more positive message than being different from the world. Their messages usually focused on real life. They understood that God promises fulfillment, satisfaction of our deepest desires, and the joy that everyone seeks. Christianity was often explained in psychological or relational terms rather than the more traditional theological ones. There was less emphasis on being different and more stress on being fulfilled.

This alternative view was more positive. While recognizing the world's evils, these Christians accepted the purity of what God had created. Was it necessary to flee from everything? Were all people to be avoided simply because they weren't Christians? Were all activities, events, foods, and pleasures wrong simply because they were enjoyable? Did God really expect us to repudiate what He'd made? After all, He entrusted creation to human beings, and surely He expects us to appreciate it.

What role do you think separation from the world plays in a holy life?

To what extent should believers associate with the world?

This new way of looking at the Christian life tended to accept people for their Christian commitment without dividing over minor issues. It also brought serious challenges to the previous theology of holiness.

These tensions weren't new. A reading of history reveals a deep concern for responsible Christian living. Early Christian thinkers devoted countless hours to developing proper convictions about life and holiness. Some resorted to external lists and activity-oriented approaches, while others were more inner and personal. The fact is that Christians differ in their approach to holy lives, and they always have.

How are we to live holy lives and still experience the joy and freedom of Christ? The only solid foundation is God Himself, as revealed in His Word. Spiritual equilibrium comes from embracing what doesn't change and applying it to life situations that constantly change.

There are many approaches to holiness. Some come directly from human experiences, some from contemporary philosophy or psychology, and some from theology. There are also different attitudes about the Bible's application to contemporary thinking on personal transformation. One approach begins with prevailing philosophies, psychologies, or theologies and quotes Bible verses to prove that so-called secular ideas may really be biblical. This often amounts to baptizing non-Christian ideas and seeking to demonstrate biblical support by proof texting. The other approach begins with Scripture, seeking to systematize its teachings apart from the prevailing theories of the secular world. Adherents of this approach may or may not use contemporary cultural language to connect the Bible and secular theories. Sometimes advocates of this approach believe others corrupt the faith by using secular language.

Either approach can be misguided. Using the language of a prevailing culture (English, for example) to explain Christian living may reveal a lack of serious understanding of Scripture and theology. In its worst form it may be nothing more than secular thinking expressed through biblical language. Biblical integrity goes far deeper than using theological words to express concepts. Besides, contemporary language sometimes expresses biblical truths quite adequately and clearly. On the other hand, expressing biblical theology with nonbiblical language, at worst, may be trendy and fail to have biblical depth.

The practical difference between the two approaches became apparent to me many years ago. I team taught a college Sunday School class with one of the local professors of psychology at the university. From all I observed, he was a model Christian. One Sunday he introduced the lesson with this question: "Are people good or bad?" The 175 college students in the room didn't know how to answer his question. He tried to promote thought and discussion by posing the question with more theological relevance: "What does the Bible say?"

"The Bible says people are bad!" So he wrote *Bible* and *bad* on one end of the chalkboard.

"What does psychology say?"

"Psychology says people are good!" He wrote *psychology* and *good* on the other end of the board. Suddenly a light dawned in his thinking. He realized he'd identified one of the most difficult of all issues: the relationship between Scripture and modern thought. Quickly he responded, "Well, we can't get into that!" and moved on with his lesson.

> *Do you agree or disagree with the generalizations that the Bible says people are bad and psychology says people are good? Why?*

Actually, the dichotomy between the two wasn't totally accurate. The Bible doesn't say human beings are bad, as many commonly understand the word. It says everyone is sinful and that being bad comes from sinfulness. On the other hand, not all psychologists would say people are good. Some recognize the innate tendency to sin. Nevertheless, the differences between the Bible and many psychological theories exist. For this reason Christians need to develop solid biblical principles of holiness as the only foundation for living a life acceptable to God.

In this study I'll provide an overview of what God says about holiness in the Scriptures. I'll also take a functional approach that assumes the practical nature of holiness. The goal is to find a balance between the theology of holiness and the biblical teaching on how to become holy. Holiness requires changes in life. Unless we understand this, holiness doesn't relate to our lives.

> *Stop and ask God to reveal specific areas in your life that require change as you continue this study. Record anything He shows you. Ask Him to help you address these areas of change and move toward a more holy life.*

Holiness is a controversial subject. My goal is to provide information leading to serious reflection, informed discussion, and better Christian living. As you read and complete the activities, open your heart to God's work in your heart, your mind, and your life. Ask Him to make you more holy by transforming you into the likeness of Jesus Christ.

This book is divided into three sections.

1. In section 1 I attempt to define *holiness,* to explore the biblical definitions, and to present major evangelical theologies of sanctification.

2. In section 2 I consider the process of life transformation. With a focus on practical, biblical teaching, I present the process of how to become holy.

3. Finally, in section 3 I focus on achieving the goal of complete holiness. In chapter 6 you'll find a brief description of complete holiness and guidance for reaching it.

Let's begin by looking at God's expectations for His people's holiness.

GOD EXPECTS HOLINESS

God expects people to be holy. The absolute bedrock of Christian living is holiness. This expectation is based on God's holy nature. The Bible frequently describes God as holy, and the biblical presentation of God's holiness is positive rather than negative. God's desire for us is for our own good. Christian living involves holiness because Christians should be like God Himself.

GOD IS HOLY

Perhaps the most fundamental principle of the universe is God's holiness. His holiness explains how He can reign in righteousness, unaffected by the evil that influences His creation. When the power of God is manifest, it's often associated with His holiness. God's intervention in the affairs of life is always redemptive or corrective, with moral implications properly associated with holiness. Because He is holy, He always wills what's right. Therefore, the relationship between God and people is based on holiness.

God's holiness permeates both the Old and New Testaments. In the Old Testament the Hebrew word translated *holy* is *qadosh,* meaning *apartness* or *sacredness.* It properly describes God but can also be used of things or places dedicated to God. In this sense the word describes the temple, refers to the biblically commanded sacrifices, and characterizes the furniture of the temple as well. The Bible makes clear that when things belong to God, they're set apart to honor Him. They're holy. Sometimes the adjective form of the word occurs, identifying God's power and majesty as being separate or apart. God is separate from humans as well. When we think of God's holiness, the most common thought is how different He is from us. He's above human frailty, impurity, and sin.

Read the following verses and record what they teach about God's holiness.

Exodus 3:5-6

Leviticus 11:44

Psalm 22:3

GOD EXPECTS US TO BE HOLY

God's holiness calls for human holiness. The Old Testament contains many examples of God's delighting in His relationships with holy people. The Bible teaches that no one can have a relationship with God without holiness. The story of redemption is the story of holiness lost and gained.

God created us to be holy. The creation accounts reveal that we're made "in His own image" (Gen. 1:27). Although theologians debate the precise meaning of the *imagio dei*—the image of God in us—one aspect of it is clear: human beings have a moral capacity. We have the ability to choose right and wrong. In the garden of Eden, Adam and Eve had experienced only good, yet they had the capacity to experience both good and evil. God created human beings in such a way that we can choose the kind of life we wish to live.

The first choice made in recorded history was a choice by Adam and Eve against God. It was a decision that introduced sin into the world, tainting every subsequent decision any person would make. The decision meant the world seems to revolve around me and my life rather than around God and His will.

How does sin interfere with your efforts to live a holy life?

The reality of human sin provides the key to understanding the remainder of the Bible. God created us to have an intimate relationship with Him. Because we're created that way, the only way to achieve ultimate personal fulfillment is to live as God intends. Yet sin distorts everything about us so that we can't understand God's ways.

Immediately after the fall, God began to reveal redemption. In Genesis 3:15 God promised a Savior from the descendants of Eve. This Messiah, Jesus, would defeat Satan. In His victory sin would also be defeated, allowing people who trust Jesus to regain the holiness lost by the original fall into sin. Theologians differ about how closely sanctification and conversion should be linked. All agree, however, that there's no possibility of personal holiness without a relationship with Jesus Christ, the Messiah. Genuine knowledge of Christ involves the mind and the heart. The mind accepts the truths about Jesus that must be correctly understood for salvation. The heart embraces Jesus in an all-encompassing, trusting relationship.

How does knowing Jesus enable you to live a holy life?

In the final analysis the Bible is about being holy. The Bible teaches us to become what God wills for us. Today we often use different terminology to explain what that means. Today it's common to hear terms like *self-actualization, self-fulfillment, happiness,* and *contentment*. These descriptive phrases have something in common. All of them basically explain what God means by the term *holiness*. We humans approach life from a self-centered, fragmented perspective. We talk about the need for personal satisfaction. In contrast, the Bible holistically approaches life from God's perspective. The Bible explains that experiences like personal satisfaction, fulfillment, and contentment come as by-products of holiness—but not before or without it. The more we're holy, the more we're satisfied, because personal fulfillment comes from being holy like God.

OLD TESTAMENT TEACHING

In the Old Testament God revealed His plan to redeem people from sin. He presented His plan in direct teaching and with pictures for our understanding. Although the central theme of the Old Testament is redemption, much Old Testament history describes the development of the nation Israel. The reason is given in Genesis 3:15:

> I will put hostility between you and the woman, and between your
> seed and her seed. He will strike your head, and you will strike his heel.
>
> **GENESIS 3:15**

God spoke these words when He first approached Adam and Eve after their sin. In that verse He predicted the course of human history. History would involve a battle in which

Satan would bruise the heel of God's Redeemer, but God's Redeemer would crush the head of Satan. The Redeemer would be human, the offspring of Eve. Although history often seems haphazard to us, the Bible explains that God works through it all.

History is intertwined with theology. God chose the nation Israel to be the vehicle of His redemption. The leaders of the young nation responded to God's call, knowing that God would use them and their offspring to bless the world with the Messiah. As God's special agents, they also realized their great responsibility to reveal the true God to the world. They were to be holy as God is holy.

DIRECT TEACHINGS OF THE OLD TESTAMENT

The Old Testament clearly and directly expresses God's call to holiness. After God delivered the nation from Egypt and gave it a government through Moses and the Ten Commandments, He inspired Moses to write the first five books of the Bible. One of those books is Leviticus.

The theme of Leviticus is holiness. The book contains 20 percent of all uses of the word in the Old Testament. The phrase "Be holy because I am holy" (11:44) is generally considered the theme of Leviticus, even though it occurs only one time in the book and only once in the entire Old Testament. It succinctly explains God's will for His people, and it provides the rationale for the entire message of Leviticus. As a microcosm of Old Testament teaching, Leviticus clearly teaches that God is holy and that His people must strive for holiness as well.

Why did God place so much importance on the holiness of His people?

Often God introduced Himself as the Holy One. The title occurs 50 times in 48 different verses of the Old Testament. The self-description implies that God alone is holy and that His holiness stands as one of the primary characteristics of Israel's God. Thus, Israel was to appreciate and worship God and to emulate His holiness.

OLD TESTAMENT PICTURES

The Old Testament clarifies the implications of God's holiness by describing how people are to relate to their holy God. These implications occur especially in passages where God disclosed the standards of holiness for those who would serve and worship Him.

Again, the Book of Leviticus serves as the focus of this discussion because it's an instruction book for worship practices. Three kinds of instruction provided information for God's people of that day: standards for those who serve God, standards for the sacrificial animals, and standards for the sacrificial rituals. These standards not only help us picture God's holiness but also reinforce the priority of holiness in relating to God.

STANDARDS FOR THOSE WHO SERVE GOD. Sometimes people assume God is unfair, especially to those who don't live up to His standards. This is hardly the case. The fact is that God instructed His people in accordance with His nature. His holy nature demands the best from those who serve Him.

These standards can be observed in the qualifications for the priesthood. By law the priesthood was limited to those of the family of Levi, the Levites. Because the Levites didn't receive an inheritance of land like the other tribes, their inheritance was the priesthood (see Deut. 10:8-9). However, not all Levites actually served as priests. Aaron and his sons were anointed with oil as priests, and they wore the special clothing of the priesthood (see Ex. 28–29). Additionally, the families of Eli (see 1 Sam. 14:3), Zadok (see Ezek. 40:46), and Amaziah (see Amos 7:10-17) were priests.

There were other restrictions besides family line. A priest couldn't serve if he had a physical defect (see Lev. 21:16-24). Marriage restrictions stated they could marry only a virgin of Israel and were forbidden marriage with a divorcée, a prostitute, a proselyte, or a widow (see Lev. 21:7-9,13-15). Further, they couldn't officiate in the sacrificial rituals if they were ritualistically impure or were under the influence of alcohol. They couldn't visit a cemetery, nor could they be around the dead unless they were of the immediate family (see Lev. 21:1-3).

The higher restrictions placed on the priests were because of their high calling. They were expected to preserve the holiness of the tabernacle, and they represented God to the people. The priests also officiated in rituals that enabled the people to draw near to God. The high standards for the priesthood reminded the people of the necessity of holiness in order to have fellowship with God. The standards disqualified some from serving, but to lower the standard would cause an inaccurate picture of God.

What standards of holiness are expected of God's servants today?

STANDARDS FOR THE SACRIFICIAL ANIMALS. These requirements were high. The most basic requirement was that the sacrifice had to be a "clean animal" or "clean bird" (Gen. 8:20). People could sacrifice cattle, goats, sheep, doves, or pigeons (see Gen. 15:9), but camels and donkeys were forbidden, even though they were readily available.

More specific regulations were to be enforced. Male animals were preferred over females (see Lev. 1:3). Older animals, at least three years old, were preferred over the young (see 1 Sam. 1:24), and the sacrificial animals were to be as physically perfect as possible (see Lev. 1:3; 3:1). The priests examined the animals to guarantee that they fulfilled these requirements.

These requirements pictured God as holy. They also reminded the people that holiness is a prerequisite for worship, for fellowship with God, and for bringing sacrifices. Israel knew they were to bring the best for God. Everything about the sacrificial system spoke against the idea that just anything would suffice for God.

What types of offerings are acceptable to God today? Why?

STANDARDS FOR THE SACRIFICIAL RITUALS. Generally, there were six steps in the process of the sacrifices. Although they differed somewhat, depending on the specific nature of the sacrifice, the pattern is instructive.

1. The worshiper brought the sacrifice to the altar, symbolizing the desire to draw near to God.

2. The worshiper laid his hand or hands on the sacrificial animal. This symbolic act reminded the sacrificer of the intimate connection between the animal to be sacrificed and the one who offered it. The animal represented the person offering it. With hands on the animal, the worshiper confessed his sins if it was a sin offering. In confession the worshiper acknowledged that sin must be taken seriously, and the death of the animal symbolically brought forgiveness.

3. In the case of animal sacrifices, the worshiper personally slaughtered the animal. The personal participation allowed the individual to assume responsibility for the sin that caused the animal's death.

4. The priest took the blood from the animal and carefully sprinkled it on the altar to symbolize cleansing.

5. Most sacrifices included burning parts of the animal. This practice represented offering God both the inside and outside of the animal.

6. Much of the meat of the offering was eaten. Sometimes the worshiper ate with the priests, but most often the priests and their families shared the meat.

How does the Old Testament sacrificial system help you understand your responsibility for your sin?

How does it help you understand Jesus' sacrifice for your sin?

This overview of the sacrificial system provides insight into the holy God's expectations. Because people are unholy, the ritualistic and symbolic cleansing reminded the people of the seriousness of their sin. The sacrifice also taught them that it was necessary to offer a perfect life to atone for sin. When the worshiper personally participated in the ritual, he expressed a sense of personal need. Worshipers accepted responsibility for their sins and for bringing their best to God. Nothing less would do.

The last book of the Old Testament called the people to holiness. Malachi warned the people about bringing sick and weak animals for sacrifice (see Mal. 1:8-14). He decried the sinful living of the priests (see 2:1-9) and deplored the generally unholy way people cared for their land.

The Old Testament consistently develops several themes:

- God is holy. Holiness is essential to His character.

- People are sinful and therefore unholy. Sin separates us from God and makes it impossible to have a relationship with God on our own. God's holiness means that He can have fellowship only with those who share His holiness. God's holiness is also the basis of His justice.

- It's possible to relate to God through the intervention of a substitute who gave up His life to make this relationship possible. The animal sacrifices pictured the One who would die and through His death provide life. Prophetically, they pictured God's provision of salvation through Jesus Christ.

Which of the three previous Old Testament themes is most meaningful to you today? Why?

NEW TESTAMENT TEACHING

Like the Old Testament, the New Testament develops the concept of holiness. Once again, it provides both direct statements and images that call us to holiness.

DIRECT TEACHINGS OF THE NEW TESTAMENT

In the New Testament three word groups refer to the idea of being holy. The most commonly used word group contains the Greek word *hagios,* which is the most frequent and the most important for our study.[2] Normally, the noun is translated as *holy* or *sacred.* The other most common words in the group are translated as *make holy, consecrate, sanctify* and *holiness, consecration, sanctification.*[3]

The New Testament uses these words in a slightly different way than the Old Testament does. For example, the words describe God much less frequently. Also, the words aren't used primarily in the temple and sacrificial arenas. Instead, they're more often associated with people. This follows a common fulfillment motif in the Old Testament that the temple and sacrifices pointed to a coming Messiah. So while the Old Testament restricted the primary use of *holy* to priests and others who serviced the temple, the New Testament applies it to all believers in Christ.

All Persons of the Trinity are called holy in the New Testament. God the Father has a holy name, an exact equivalent to calling His Person holy (see Luke 1:49). God the Son, Jesus, is called holy in multiple places by demons (see Mark 1:24), by Peter in his confession of Jesus' death (see John 6:69), and by Peter in his public preaching (see Acts 4:27). God the Spirit has the attribute of holiness associated with His name. He's most often called the Holy Spirit. Each Person of the Trinity is to be set apart, honored, and worshiped as holy.

The New Testament indicates that the entire Trinity shapes us toward holiness. Bible students recognize the distinctive work of each Person of the Trinity in our salvation. God the Father chooses, God the Son accomplishes salvation, and God the Holy Spirit applies it to our lives so that we come to Christ. Each Person of the Trinity has a unique task in accomplishing God's plan. Even so, the New Testament identifies each Person of the Trinity with our holiness. Paul prayed for the Thessalonians that God the Father would "sanctify you completely" (1 Thess. 5:23), having said earlier that sanctification was "God's will" for them (4:3). Speaking to the Corinthians, Paul explained that because of God the Father's work, "You are in Christ Jesus, who became God-given wisdom for us—our righteousness, sanctification, and redemption" (1 Cor. 1:30).

At conversion Jesus is our sanctification. Sanctification is also a joint work of the Son and the Holy Spirit. Contrasting the Christian lifestyle with that of unbelievers, Paul reminded the Corinthians, "You were washed, you were sanctified, you were justified in the name of the Lord Jesus Christ and by the Spirit of our God" (1 Cor. 6:11). Finally, sanctification can be described as the work of the Holy Spirit both in bringing us to salvation (see 1 Pet. 1:1-2) and in working God's purity in us (see 1 Thess. 4:7-8).

> *What's your response to the reality that all three Persons of the Trinity played a role in your salvation and are involved in your ongoing sanctification?*

> *How are you cooperating with the work of Jesus and the Holy Spirit to bring about spiritual growth in your life?*

NEW TESTAMENT PICTURES

The New Testament encourages holiness by using metaphors that describe the identity of believers. In the Old Testament holiness was centered in the temple. The temple was dedicated to God, the sacrifices had to be holy, and the priests and Levites had a higher responsibility to live holy lives. In the New Testament these three aspects of the temple and its activity are applied to Christians.

CHRISTIANS ARE THE NEW TEMPLE. Believers have the responsibility of displaying God's attributes. Jesus anticipated this responsibility in His ministry. When questioned about His authority for chasing moneychangers from the temple, He pointed to His own resurrection but implied a time when the temple would no longer be needed (see John 2:19-22). When the Samaritan woman questioned Jesus about the best place to worship, Jesus responded that the time had come when the place didn't matter. With Jesus' arrival on earth, it was more important to know *how* to worship than *where* to worship. Those who "worship in spirit and truth" (John 4:24) will truly worship the Father. Paul had this truth in mind when he encouraged the Corinthian Christians to holy living:

We are the sanctuary of the living God, as God said:
"I will dwell among them and walk among them, and
I will be their God, and they will be My people."

2 CORINTHIANS 6:16

CHRISTIANS ARE THE NEW SACRIFICE. In Romans 12:1-2 Paul used terminology from the temple's sacrificial system to explain how we're to relate to our holy God:

I urge you to present your bodies as a living sacrifice, holy and pleasing to God; this is your spiritual worship. Do not be conformed to this age, but be transformed by the renewing of your mind, so that you may discern what is the good, pleasing, and perfect will of God.

ROMANS 12:1-2

We're to present our bodies to God with the same care of ourselves that the Old Testament saint gave to selecting and offering a sacrificial animal. The sacrifices for sin to gain mercy in the Old Testament are replaced by our offering ourselves to God because of His mercy.

CHRISTIANS ARE GOD'S PRIESTS. The apostle Peter emphasized this truth to his readers, who, being Jewish, understood the significance of the temple rituals. He explained that we Christians "are a chosen race, a royal priesthood, a holy nation, a people for His possession" (1 Pet. 2:9). This verse originally applied to the nation Israel but now to Christians as God's special representatives. In addition, earlier in this single passage Peter used all three of the images we've discussed to remind Christians of our calling:

You yourselves, as living stones, are being built into a spiritual house for a holy priesthood to offer spiritual sacrifices acceptable to God through Jesus Christ.

1 PETER 2:5

Equating believers with the sacred rituals of Israel reminds us of God's high and holy calling on our lives.

Evaluate the extent to which your life demonstrates the New Testament pictures of holiness.

1	2	3	4	5	6	7	8	9	10
Ignoring God's presence   *Worshiping in spirit and truth*

1	2	3	4	5	6	7	8	9	10
Conformed to the world   *Offering myself as a living sacrifice*

1	2	3	4	5	6	7	8	9	10
Living for myself   *Representing God*

The New Testament presents two major points about holiness.

1. Holiness identifies whatever is holy as separate from the world.

2. Holiness challenges believers to become holy, separate from the sinfulness of the world.

THE GOAL OF HOLINESS: TO BE LIKE JESUS

The New Testament teaches holiness in many of the same ways as the Old Testament. We observed that people are created in the image of God. The New Testament continues the themes of the distortion of the image of God and the possibility of God's restoring His image in believers.

The most direct teaching on the fulfillment of the image of God in Christians occurs in Paul's prison epistles, Ephesians and Colossians. In Colossians Paul spoke to the church about personal purity:

> Do not lie to one another, since you have put off the old self with its practices and have put on the new self. You are being renewed in knowledge according to the image of your Creator.
>
> **COLOSSIANS 3:9-10**

The goal for a new person in Christ, "the new self," is to be "renewed in knowledge according to the image of your Creator" (v. 10).

The New Testament consistently describes Jesus as the Creator and as the image of God (see John 1:1-4; Heb. 1:1-3). Paul stated:

He is the image of the invisible God, the firstborn over all creation. Everything was created by Him, in heaven and on earth, the visible and the invisible, whether thrones or dominions or rulers or authorities—all things have been created through Him and for Him.

COLOSSIANS 1:15-16

Jesus brings to us all God is. The goal of holiness is to be like Jesus:

Those He foreknew He also predestined to be conformed to the image of His Son.

ROMANS 8:29; ALSO SEE 1 CORINTHIANS 15:49;
2 CORINTHIANS 3:18; PHILIPPIANS 3:21

The New Testament makes the Old Testament teaching concrete, understandable, and manageable. Jesus is the image of God. The Epistle to the Hebrews expresses this unmistakenly. Hebrews 1:3 says Jesus is "the radiance of God's glory and the exact expression of His nature." Jesus is the One who makes God the Father visible and who brings God's presence and blessings to earth. Hebrews reveals that Jesus is exactly God; no one is like Him. But if we can live like Him, we will have fulfilled God's expectations.

What emotions do you feel when you read that God expects you to be like Jesus?

Spend time in prayer about your personal holiness. Ask God to show you ways you need to be separate from the world. Express your desire to be holy and to be formed into the image of Christ. Ask for His transforming power and work in your life.

---

1. Scott Underwood, "Holiness," in *15 Songs Proclaiming His Holiness* (Vineyard Music Group, 1998).
2. The second word is *ieros,* which occurs very infrequently in the New Testament. It refers to what is consecrated by God's power. The word basically means something is intrinsically holy. It refers to the "sacred Scriptures" (2 Tim. 3:15), and its neuter form almost always refers to the temple (see Matt. 4:5), meaning Herod's temple. As might be expected, it occurs primarily in the Gospels with a literal meaning. The third word group is represented by the noun *osios.* This word, which occurs less than a dozen times in the New Testament, is usually a quotation from the Greek translation of the Old Testament, the Septuagint.
3. Horst Seebass, "Holy, Consecrate, Sanctify, Saints, Devout," in *The New International Dictionary of New Testament Theology,* vol. 2, ed. Colin Brown (Grand Rapids, MI: Zondervan Publishing House, 1976), 223–38.

CHAPTER 1 GROUP EXPERIENCE
HOLINESS—GOOD FOR ALL OF US

COMING TOGETHER

1. *After introducing yourselves, share thoughts and images that come to mind when you hear the word* holy.

2. *As a group, create a biblical definition of* holiness.

ATTITUDES TOWARD HOLINESS

1. *How would you describe our society's attitudes toward holiness and toward people who want to be holy? Why do you think society views holiness this way?*

2. *To what extent should believers separate themselves from their culture in an effort to live holy lives? Why?*

3. *What problems can result when Christians reduce holiness to a set of do's and don'ts? Why?*

GOD EXPECTS HOLINESS

1. *What does the Bible mean when it says God is holy?*

2. *Read Genesis 1:27.*

> God created man in His own image;
> He created him in the image of God;
> He created them male and female.

What does it mean to be made in the image of God?

Does being made in the image of God automatically make us holy? Why or why not?

3. *Read the following verses.*

I am Yahweh your God, so you must consecrate yourselves and be holy because I am holy.

LEVITICUS 11:44

As the One who called you is holy, you also are to be holy in all your conduct; for it is written, "Be holy, because I am holy."

1 PETER 1:15-16

Why is it important for God's people to be holy?

OLD TESTAMENT TEACHING

1. *How does the Old Testament sacrificial system reflect God's holiness?*

2. *How does the Old Testament sacrificial system demand holiness of those who wish to approach God?*

3. *What applications can you identify in the Old Testament sacrificial system for people today who want to be holy?*

NEW TESTAMENT TEACHING

1. The New Testament calls not only the three Persons of the Trinity holy but also all Christians. How can believers be holy?

2. Read the following verses.

Do you not know that your body is a temple of the Holy Spirit, who is in you, whom you have received from God? You are not your own; you were bought at a price. Therefore honor God with your body.

1 CORINTHIANS 6:19-20, NIV

We are the sanctuary of the living God, as God said:
>I will dwell among them
>and walk among them,
>and I will be their God,
>and they will be My people.

2 CORINTHIANS 6:16

In what ways are Christians the temple of God? How does this description call us to holiness?

3. Read Romans 12:1-2.

I urge you to present your bodies as a living sacrifice, holy and pleasing to God; this is your spiritual worship. Do not be conformed to this age, but be transformed by the renewing of your mind, so that you may discern what is the good, pleasing, and perfect will of God.

How can Christians be living sacrifices? How does this description call us to holiness?

4. Read 1 Peter 2:5,9.

You yourselves, as living stones, are being built into a
spiritual house for a holy priesthood to offer spiritual
sacrifices acceptable to God through Jesus Christ.
   You are a chosen race, a royal priesthood,
   a holy nation, a people for His possession,
   so that you may proclaim the praises
   of the One who called you out of darkness
   into His marvelous light.

*In what ways are Christians God's priests? How does this description call us
to holiness?*

THE GOAL OF HOLINESS: TO BE LIKE JESUS

1. Read Romans 8:29 and Colossians 3:9-10.

Those He foreknew He also predestined to be
conformed to the image of His Son.

Do not lie to one another, since you have put off the old self
with its practices and have put on the new self. You are being
renewed in knowledge according to the image of your Creator.

*How do these verses change your idea of holiness? What is the goal
of holiness?*

2. What's your response to the expectation that you become like Jesus?

*3. End the session by praying that through this study, God will show you ways
you need to grow in holiness and will place you on a path of continual growth
in the likeness of Jesus.*

CHAPTER 2
THE MEANING OF HOLINESS

A man had received a ticket for speeding. When the judge asked how he pleaded, he started into a long, progressively louder monologue about why he wasn't guilty. His defense was simple: "Your honor, I'm a holy man, and I can't sin. I wasn't speeding." The people in the courtroom began to laugh, causing the man to give his defense even louder. Finally, to preserve order in the court, the judge stated, "Don't do it again! Dismissed!" All the way out the door, the man shouted, "I'm a holy, righteous man, and I can't sin."

Many questions arise about what personal holiness actually means. In this chapter I hope to clarify some of the basic theological terminology, as well as to briefly explore the major evangelical approaches to holy living. *Holiness* overlaps *sanctification,* so the words are practically interchangeable. A biblical survey of the uses of these terms places the focus on being made holy at conversion and being made completely holy in glory. Nevertheless, at times the word *holiness* clearly conveys an ongoing sense of sanctification.[1] Many theologians make the words *holiness* and *sanctification* synonymous. Throughout this book I use the two almost synonymously.

THE DIMENSIONS OF HOLINESS

The Bible identifies different dimensions of holiness. From one perspective sanctification occurs immediately at conversion. From another it requires constant attention and progressively produces complete transformation. All believers feel a constant tendency toward sin and in reflective moments realize that throughout life we need to grow in personal holiness.

How does your life illustrate the two dimensions of holiness—occurring immediately at conversion and progressively taking place over time?

IMMEDIATE POSITIONAL HOLINESS

At conversion we are complete in Christ. At that time God guarantees us all the blessings eternal life brings. He views us through the lens of Jesus, so each time He relates to us, He recognizes our relationship to His Son. The relationship between the believer and Christ enables God to consider Jesus' experiences as those of the believer.

WE'RE FORGIVEN. The Bible teaches that at conversion we identify with Jesus' life and death. God places our sins on Jesus so that His death pays the price for our sin. We stand before God clean, without sin, because through Jesus, God forgives our sins—past, present, and future. We enter a right relationship with God. He therefore always sees us as intimately associated with Jesus, for in Jesus' death we too died, and in His resurrection we were raised to new life. The apostle Paul described it this way:

Are you unaware that all of us who were baptized into Christ Jesus were baptized into His death? Therefore we were buried with Him by baptism into death, in order that, just as Christ was raised from the dead by the glory of the Father, so we too may walk in a new way of life. For if we have been joined with Him in the likeness of His death, we will certainly also be in the likeness of His resurrection.

ROMANS 6:3-5

Describe in your own words what it means to identify with Jesus' life and death.

WE'RE MADE RIGHTEOUS. At conversion God also considers Jesus' righteousness as ours. When God sees Jesus' life as ours, He treats us the same way He treats Jesus. From this perspective He considers us as completely holy. Just as Jesus never sinned, so in God's eyes we've never sinned. God can bless us with the good things of eternal life because He no longer sees our sins that He forgave in Jesus' death. And He no longer sees our failures, because He sees us connected to Jesus' life.

Paul based this truth on the life of David. Though David was a sinner, he experienced the blessings of a right relationship with God. Paul quoted Psalm 32:1-2:

David also speaks of the blessing of the man God
credits righteousness to apart from works:
> How joyful are those whose lawless acts are
> forgiven and whose sins are covered! How joyful
> is the man the Lord will never charge with sin!

ROMANS 4:6-8

*What emotions do you experience when you read that because you're
a believer in Jesus, God will never count your sins against you?*

These complementary perspectives on forgiveness and righteousness reveal a great truth about our salvation. From the moment of conversion God sees us as holy. We stand before Him completely holy, our sins forgiven and put away by God. The recognition of this truth allowed Paul to relate to the Corinthian church from the perspective of their relationship with God. The Corinthian church was the most problem-ridden and sinful church of the New Testament era, yet Paul wrote:

> To the church of God in Corinth, to those sanctified
> in Christ Jesus and called to be holy.
>
> **1 CORINTHIANS 1:2, NIV**

Surely this church occupied more of the apostle's time and energy than any other church we know of. Scholars generally conclude that Paul made at least three visits to Corinth to help establish and strengthen the church. Additionally, Paul wrote at least four letters to the church in Corinth. One preceded 1 Corinthians (see 1 Cor. 5:9, which refers to a previous letter). He wrote another letter between what we now know as 1 and 2 Corinthians. It was a harsh letter dealing with a matter of church discipline (see 2 Cor. 7:8, which is generally understood to refer to a letter after 1 Cor.). Yet he introduced his epistle to these believers by calling them sanctified.

First Corinthians reveals anything but a holy people. The church was divided into parties, and the church refused to take a stand against blatant, publicly acknowledged immorality. Relationships among Christians deteriorated to the point that believers actually sought legal action from the state to resolve issues between themselves and other members. They had theological problems with the exercise of spiritual gifts, questions about marriage, and divisions at the Lord's Supper as well as the accompanying Agape Feast. The church hardly seemed sanctified.

Yet Paul confidently approached the Corinthian believers because of their relationship with Christ. Though they sinned, they were in Christ. Therefore, they were sanctified. God saw them as His people, pure enough that He could relate to them as His own. No biblical text so clearly expresses the truth that at conversion God sees us differently. He no longer looks at us and sees the enormity of our sin. He sees us as completely holy because of the life and death of Jesus.

Do you see yourself as holy? Why or why not?

The letter to the Ephesians confirms the same truth. In praying for the church and hoping they'd experience the magnificence of God's power, Paul said:

> That power is like the working of his mighty strength, which he
> exerted in Christ when he raised him from the dead and seated
> him at his right hand in the heavenly realms, far above all rule
> and authority, power and dominion, and every title that can be
> given, not only in the present age but also in the one to come.

EPHESIANS 1:19-21, NIV

Thus, Paul related the Ephesians' spiritual position to the same power that raised Jesus from the dead.

In chapter 2 the same description fits believers. There Paul stated:

> God, who is rich in mercy, because of His great love that He
> had for us, made us alive with the Messiah even though we
> were dead in trespasses. You are saved by grace! Together with
> Christ Jesus He also raised us up and seated us in the heavens,
> so that in the coming ages He might display the immeasurable
> riches of His grace through His kindness to us in Christ Jesus.

EPHESIANS 2:4-7

Both Jesus and the believer are raised from the dead and seated in the heavenly realms. If believers are already seated in the heavenly realms because of our identification with Christ, it's clear that God sees us and treats us as already holy.

Theologians often call this standing with God positional or legal holiness. Both terms attempt to express what's true about us but isn't fully realized in our experience. *Positional holiness,* preferred by many, describes a situation that's different from what we normally think about ourselves. Based on our thoughts and behavior, we wouldn't see ourselves as holy. Yet God placed us in a position of holiness in Christ, and He views us that way.

Legal holiness, a term that's preferred by others, recognizes a true condition based on the pronouncement of a judge. It comes from Paul's term *justification. Justification* means God pronounces a believer justified or righteous. The term says nothing about our actual condition. In fact, believers are guilty and deserve punishment. But when the Judge, God, pronounces us justified, that ruling prevails. Describing something as legal adequately conveys the truth of God's perspective. The Judge can declare us justified because of our identification with Christ.

What's your reaction to the idea that God has declared you holy and justified?

At conversion something real happens. A believer is set apart for God. Yet more seems to happen when God sets us apart. We're changed. Our lives may not immediately display the completeness of character we hope we'll have, but we have new desires and directions. Being set apart brings with it the desire to live in a manner consistent with being set apart by God as holy.

Similarly, positional holiness means God declares us holy. It doesn't refer to the way we live. It refers to what God says about our spiritual state, based on our identification with Christ. This positional holiness enables God to speak with us, to bring strength to us, to cause us to grow in Christian virtues, and to use us in His service.

The focus of this book is to define *holiness* biblically and to describe a holy life. Chapters 3–5 will describe what being set apart to God looks like. They'll discuss the intuitive changes at conversion that each individual will live out after receiving at conversion the desire to fulfill the righteous standards of God's Word.

What desires and values changed after you were saved?

CONTINUING PROGRESSIVE HOLINESS

The second dimension of holiness is called progressive holiness. Even though we're set apart to God, we often fail as we struggle to overcome the habits of sinful behavior. The truth that we're already seen as holy encourages us as we seek to become holy.

More Scriptures apply to everyday living—to progressive holiness—than to our position before God. Most of the epistles contain passages about how to implement the theology of conversion. God knows we have personal problems, sins, social prejudices, and religious questions. These require us to grow into what God expects for righteous living. Actually, Christians hope to become better for good reasons.

WE'RE MADE IN GOD'S IMAGE. Because we're created in the image of God, every person has a sense of right and wrong just by virtue of being human. The knowledge that we all share the same desire should be an encouragement in our individual pursuits of holiness. When people of any society reason together to formulate standards of behavior, they act on an inner sense of rightness that guides them. Paul called this the law of God "written on [our] hearts" (Rom. 2:14-15). The human laws we construct simply reveal God's higher standards. At conversion God's Holy Spirit builds on our natural moral instinct, giving it a more significant place in our lives and directing it toward the purposes of God. The Holy Spirit urges believers to become what God originally intended us to be.

WE'RE SAVED FOR HOLINESS. Even the basic elements of conversion encourage us toward holiness. Several things incline people to accept Christ. We must have a sense of sinfulness. Consciousness of sin brings a realization of our separation from God. In addition, a proper understanding of sin brings the knowledge that sin keeps us from realizing our full potential. Sin encourages us to act in ways we'd rather not, and it produces patterns of living that harm others and ourselves. This twofold understanding—that sin offends God and damages us—produces in us a deep desire to escape sin. Who wouldn't want to change a life that brings God's judgment and at the same time causes great pain?

This understanding then leads to repentance. The Greek word for repentance is *metanoia,* meaning *to change one's attitude.* Many times we hear that *repentance* means *to change one's mind,* but the Greek word *noia* refers to a much deeper concept. It connotes attitudes and dispositions. Repentance drives people to the attitude that they'll do anything to change and stop sinning.

How did the Holy Spirit convict you of sin, creating a desire to repent?

The more deeply we analyze our life patterns and values, the more we realize we can't change our attitudes to honor God. We need help. The desire to change prompts the cry for a Savior. That makes the gospel good news! God says we don't need to change our attitudes by ourselves, nor can we change the patterns of our lives by ourselves. Further, there's nothing we can do by ourselves to escape God's wrath, which will be directed toward sin. No matter how much right we do, we can't erase the wrong already done. It forever stands between God and us until we accept Jesus Christ. We need forgiveness of the past because we can do nothing to change it. The forgiveness offered by Jesus Christ brings the power we need to live holy lives.

Building on the conversion experience, the Bible consistently encourages Christians to be holy. Many New Testament passages teach Christians about practical holiness. The epistles generally fall into a pattern. The first chapters discuss certain theological issues a church was wrestling with, while the last chapters apply those theologies to the Christian life. In the broadest sense all of the practical passages in the epistles encourage us in holiness because they call us to conform to God's values.

In many passages Paul urged Christians to live holy lives. For example, he used active commands to reinforce the necessity of obedience in Romans 6:

> *Do not let* sin reign in your mortal body so that you obey its desires.
> And *do not offer* any parts of it to sin as weapons for unrighteousness.
> But as those who are alive from the dead, *offer* yourselves to God,
> and all the parts of yourselves to God as weapons for righteousness.
>
> **ROMANS 6:12-13, EMPHASIS ADDED**

In Galatians 5 Paul explained the importance of leaving the old life for the new:

> The acts of the sinful nature are obvious: sexual immorality,
> impurity and debauchery; idolatry and witchcraft; hatred, discord,
> jealousy, fits of rage, selfish ambition, dissensions, factions and
> envy; drunkenness, orgies, and the like. I warn you, as I did before,
> that those who live like this will not inherit the kingdom of God.
>
> **GALATIANS 5:19-21, NIV**

One of Paul's most pointed commands contrasts the way of the world with following Christ:

> Brothers, by the mercies of God, I urge you to present your
> bodies as a living sacrifice, holy and pleasing to God; this is
> your spiritual worship. Do not be conformed to this age, but
> be transformed by the renewing of your mind, so that you may
> discern what is the good, pleasing, and perfect will of God.
>
> **ROMANS 12:1-2**

Go back and underline Paul's commands in the three previous passages. How can following these commands lead to holy living?

Other writers provide similar encouragement. The apostle Peter wrote:

> Prepare your minds for action; be self-controlled; set your hope fully on the grace to be given you when Jesus Christ is revealed. As obedient children, do not conform to the evil desires you had when you lived in ignorance.
>
> **1 PETER 1:13-14, NIV**

James, the half brother of our Lord, warned:

> Submit to God. But resist the Devil, and he will flee from you. Draw near to God, and He will draw near to you. Cleanse your hands, sinners, and purify your hearts, double-minded people! Be miserable and mourn and weep. Your laughter must change to mourning and your joy to sorrow. Humble yourselves before the Lord, and He will exalt you.
>
> **JAMES 4:7-10**

John expressed this point as well:

> Do not love the world or the things that belong to the world. If anyone loves the world, love for the Father is not in him. For everything that belongs to the world—the lust of the flesh, the lust of the eyes, and the pride in one's lifestyle—is not from the Father, but is from the world. And the world with its lust is passing away, but the one who does God's will remains forever.
>
> **1 JOHN 2:15-17**

The writer of Hebrews exhorted believers to holiness as well. In Hebrews 3 he acknowledged that his readers were positionally holy:

> Holy brothers, who share in the heavenly calling, fix your thoughts
> on Jesus, the apostle and high priest whom we confess.
>
> **HEBREWS 3:1, NIV**

At the same time, he urged his readers on to practical holiness:

> See to it, brothers, that none of you has a sinful, unbelieving
> heart that turns away from the living God. But encourage
> one another daily, as long as it is called Today, so that
> none of you may be hardened by sin's deceitfulness.
>
> **HEBREWS 3:12-13, NIV**

> Make every effort to live in peace with all men and to be
> holy; without holiness no one will see the Lord.
>
> **HEBREWS 12:14, NIV**

*Go back and underline in the previous passages the exhortations that
are most meaningful in your pursuit of holiness. Why do you think these
exhortations are necessary for believers?*

These passages illustrate that God's commands to be holy permeate the entire New
Testament. The also clarify God's plan for Christians. Conversion is the beginning of a life
devoted to overcoming sin, developing new values, and growing in holiness. Because of
positional holiness God views Christians as already holy. Because of progressive holiness
Christians actually become what God intends.

ULTIMATE COMPLETE HOLINESS

God intends for believers to attain complete perfection, actually living without sin.
Positional and progressive sanctification begin this process. Although both have significant meaning for Christians, both leave us dissatisfied. Positional sanctification views us
from God's perspective, based on God's decree of justification. Progressive sanctification
describes our progress toward personal sanctification. Nevertheless, sin continues to be a

problem in life. Our hearts cry for complete freedom from sin. We long for a time when sin no longer tempts us and when we can see God without the limitations sin imposes. These longings will be rewarded. The Bible promises complete holiness.

The doctrine of complete sanctification brings comfort and hope. Even if we can't escape the influence of sin on earth, someday that will change. Complete sanctification will bring ultimate victory. Because sinfulness and finiteness limit our ability to know God as we should, complete holiness brings full knowledge and fellowship.

What's your reaction to the reality of ultimate complete holiness?

Several passages of Scripture teach this aspect of holiness. One of the clearest is 1 John 3:2:

> We are God's children now, and what we will be has not
> yet been revealed. We know that when He appears, we
> will be like Him because we will see Him as He is.
>
> **1 JOHN 3:2**

This text and others suggest important truths about complete sanctification.

RELEASE FROM SIN OCCURS AT DEATH. At that time the limitations of sin are removed, and believers immediately go to be with the Lord in a perfect place. At death believers become morally perfect. Perfect character replaces life infected with sin.

THE COMPLETION OF HOLINESS IS FUTURE. Completeness will happen when we see Jesus. No one on earth fully understands what complete sanctification will be like. Complete sanctification will come with the complete knowledge of Jesus, which will occur at the second coming.

Most Christians will be with Christ at that time, but we'll be without our bodies. Complete sanctification includes more than the soul and spirit. It extends to the body as well. In writing to the Thessalonians, Paul prayed:

May the God of peace Himself sanctify you completely.
And may your spirit, soul, and body be kept sound and
blameless for the coming of our Lord Jesus Christ.

1 THESSALONIANS 5:23

The body will be transformed when Jesus comes again; believers will leave behind the body that's naturally maintained and embrace the spiritually maintained body (see 1 Cor. 15:35-53). In the transformation process from natural to spiritual, the body is sanctified. Then God's plan for holiness reaches completion.

The body will remain in the grave until the resurrection of the body, which will occur when Jesus returns to earth. Until that time believers in heaven experience moral and spiritual holiness, but they await the joy of reunion with their glorified bodies.

Jesus' power alone effects the change into His image. The verse "We will see Him as He is" (1 John 3:2) suggests that we will be transformed by seeing Him.

Identify ways you look forward to seeing perfect holiness bring healing to the following components of your life.

Body:

Mind:

Emotions:

Spirit:

THE PROMISE OF VICTORY ENCOURAGES DAILY LIFE. The Book of Romans also teaches a future complete sanctification: "Sin will not rule over you, because you are not under law but under grace" (Rom. 6:14). This verse concludes a discussion of believers' death to sin and the command to present our bodies to God as instruments of righteousness. Obviously, ultimate victory awaits believers. The fact is, "Sin will not rule over you."

This is more than a statement of hope. It doesn't teach that if we make the correct choices, we'll gain victory over sin. It clearly states that sin won't rule over us.

Because our final destiny is a life free from sin, Paul presented this truth as an incentive to make the correct choices on earth. It is both inconceivable and inconsistent for believers to choose to follow a life of sin here on earth when our salvation promises us a life of perfection someday. The way we live our lives on earth should be consistent with our real character and destination: heaven and its perfection.

What are some obstacles to consistent holy living in your life?

Start regularly praying that God will help you overcome these obstacles with His spiritual resources.

Romans 6:14 also provides the reason for the promise of holiness: "You are not under law, but under grace." Law brings its demands, accusations, and judgments. Because no one besides Jesus has ever lived correctly under law, every person can expect to be judged as a sinner. For Paul, judgment under law and the power of sin go hand in hand: "The sting of death is sin, and the power of sin is the law" (1 Cor. 15:56). Christians have been delivered from the power of sin in their lives, and they've died to law:

> You also were put to death in relation to the law through the crucified body of the Messiah, so that you may belong to another—to Him who was raised from the dead—that we may bear fruit for God.
>
> **ROMANS 7:4**

Grace has done what the law could not do. Grace not only erases the sin of the past but also provides for the life of the future. Grace guarantees that sin will be completely defeated in a believer's life. Paul said:

> The law came along to multiply the trespass. But where sin multiplied, grace multiplied even more so that, just as sin reigned in death, so also grace will reign through righteousness, resulting in eternal life through Jesus Christ our Lord.
>
> **ROMANS 5:20-21**

Christians, now under grace, will someday receive the full blessings of salvation, including complete victory over sin.

What expressions of God's grace do you see in your life that are overcoming sin and helping you grow in holiness?

These representative texts describe the ultimate goal of being like Christ. God completes redemption at a believer's death, after the person has experienced everything God intends. We've already seen that God intends to bring believers into the fullness of the image of God. The New Testament clarifies what that means: being like Jesus. Ultimate complete holiness will finally bring us to the blessed state of Christlikeness.

In summary, holiness occurs in three stages.

1. Believers are positionally holy at conversion.

2. While living on earth, believers are expected to become progressively more holy through fellowship with Christ.

3. Finally, believers anticipate complete sanctification when the Lord returns and resurrects their bodies.

CONTEMPORARY EVANGELICAL APPROACHES TO SANCTIFICATION

Evangelical Christians have developed various theologies explaining how believers achieve holiness in personal living. I'll briefly survey four of those positions. The categories are quite broad. The particular descriptions of these approaches to holiness don't mean everyone who teaches that approach will agree on the finer points. I'm attempting to simplify for the purpose of basic understanding.[2]

THE WESLEYAN APPROACH

Wesleyan theology comes from the great preacher and theologian John Wesley. The Wesleyan tradition encompasses many church groups, such as Free Methodists, Nazarenes, the Christian and Missionary Alliance, and the Salvation Army.

This approach has been known for its focus on social issues that are viewed as an integral part of Christian faith. This emphasis lies at the heart of the Wesleyan interpretation of Christianity since, according to this theology, all mature believers demonstrate their relationship to Christ by the way they live.

Wesley believed Christians can attain complete perfection on earth. This belief corresponds to Wesley's understanding that Christians should develop personal holiness. Perhaps more significantly for this study, believers not only *should* develop it but also *can* develop it. Wesley saw the ability to attain complete perfection as the logical outworking of grace, regeneration, and faith motivated by love.

Do you believe Christians can attain perfection on earth? Why or why not?

Wesleyans believe the promise of sanctification occurs in both the Old and the New Testaments. Wesley understood that the promise involved deliverance from all willful sin, based on Old Testament passages like these:

> The LORD your God will circumcise your heart and the
> hearts of your descendants, and you will love Him with
> all your heart and all your soul so that you will live.
>
> **DEUTERONOMY 30:6**

> I will also sprinkle clean water on you, and you will be clean.
> I will cleanse you from all your impurities and all your idols.
>
> **EZEKIEL 36:25**

Wesley pointed to corollaries in the New Testament:

> What the law could not do since it was limited by the flesh, God
> did. He condemned sin in the flesh by sending His own Son in
> flesh like ours under sin's domain, and as a sin offering, in order
> that the law's requirement would be accomplished in us who
> do not walk according to the flesh but according to the Spirit.
>
> **ROMANS 8:3-4**

In this, love is perfected with us so that we may have confidence in the day of judgment, for we are as He is in this world.

1 JOHN 4:17

Wesleyans consider deliverance from sin as deliverance from any *known* sin. That is, Christians can reach a state of sinlessness regarding any *known* violation of a law. Sinless perfection doesn't include our suffering the influence of ignorance, mistakes, infirmities, and involuntary temptations.[3] To reach sinless perfection, Christians must have a crisis experience that includes a definite act of faith.

This Wesleyan tradition focuses on two experiential points in a Christian's life: justification and sanctification. These two experiences have different motivations and outworkings. Justification brings regeneration and conversion. Sanctification brings complete victory over sin.

THE PENTECOSTAL APPROACH

Pentecostalism developed into two distinct movements. The earlier grew from a Wesleyan tradition and has many similarities to the Wesleyan approach to sanctification. The second came from various traditions that don't reflect the distinctives of the Wesleyans.

The differences between the two wings of the movement basically involve one point: Can Christians live sinlessly? Those whose history includes the Wesleyan tradition argue that Christians can achieve a state of freedom from known sin. The others believe that such a state is impossible.

All Pentecostals believe in a baptism of the Holy Spirit that brings the ability to witness effectively. The pro-Wesleyan group believes the filling of the Holy Spirit comes to believers who are already mature and makes them sinless. Thus, the baptism of the Spirit is a third stage of spiritual development following conversion and sanctification. The other group believes the baptism of the Holy Spirit following conversion simply brings power for purity and for effective proclamation of the gospel.

Which Pentecostal view most closely represents your belief about the Holy Spirit's role in making believers holy? Why?

The initial evidence of the filling of the Spirit is the ability to speak in tongues, although that's only one evidence. Many Pentecostals point to Acts 2:4, which describes how the Holy Spirit came on the early church:

> All of them were filled with the Holy Spirit and began
> to speak in other tongues as the Spirit enabled them.
>
> **ACTS 2:4, NIV**

Pentecostals see speaking in tongues as normative for all believers. They say Christians today should seek the baptism of the Holy Spirit, and they'll recognize the Spirit's presence by comparing the phenomena in their lives to the experience of the church in Acts 2.

All Pentecostals agree that the baptism of the Spirit brings a new ability to become holy. No one can be what God desires without that experience.

THE KESWICK APPROACH

The Keswick teaching of holiness gets its name from a series of meetings that began in 1875 in Keswick, England. In America the term *Keswick* identifies a message often called the victorious life. Keswick beliefs can't be confined to a single denomination. The Keswick teachers were powerful, articulate persons who gained a significant following because of both their oratory and the power of their message.

Keswick theology basically teaches two stages of growth. The first is conversion. Many Christians know nothing more than conversion. They often live their lives like their non-Christian neighbors because they simply don't know anything different. As a result, average Christians are constantly overcome by temptation and sin. Such Christians are likely to live like the church in Corinth, which was carnal (worldly) or like Paul's self-description in Romans 7:14-25. Both examples express the fact that Christians can be carnal, living just like the world from which they came.

The answer to this dilemma is a second spiritual experience recognizing that Christians are dead to sin. Because of death to sin, every Christian should make a conscious act of commitment of the whole person to Christ, with a prayer of faith that God will provide victory. This theology stresses a normal Christian life, which is far from the average Christian life. The average Christian struggles, hoping to live up to the expectations that come at conversion. Through a second experience subsequent to conversion, Christians can move from average to normal. The normal Christian life brings great blessings and spiritual effectiveness.

Why do you think many believers live worldly lives without spiritual power and victory?

Which word best describes your life—average or normal? Why?

Keswick teachers presented the idea of life and death as the basis of victory. For most Keswick preachers, the way to life is death. The way to unleash the power that brings victory is to die; every believer must die to sin. This is normally interpreted as a second experience after salvation. After believers have died to sin, they should die anew by reaffirming their condition of being dead to sin. Basically, believers must get out of the way and allow Jesus to live through them. Progress in the Christian life comes by yielding to Jesus, expressed as dying to sin, and allowing Christ to live through their lives day by day. One distinguishing phrase of Keswick theologians is "Death to self; alive to God." Death to self means believers must count on the fact that they've died to sin. Further, they must live a life of obedience, normally referred to as the crucified life. The power of Christ is unleashed when believers die to sin, allowing Jesus to live through them. The two unique key terms of Keswick theology are *death* and *Christ within*.

What's your reaction to the Keswick idea of dying to sin as the key to spiritual victory?

THE REFORMED APPROACH

The Reformed tradition derives its name from John Calvin and his followers. The Reformed tradition has gained strength in the centuries since Calvin lived. However, while there were basic similarities among the Reformers, there wasn't a clear teaching on sanctification. It's difficult to identify one strain of teaching that all Reformed theologians accept, but we can identify some characteristics of the Reformed position.

REFORMED THEOLOGY DISTINGUISHES BETWEEN JUSTIFICATION AND SANCTIFICATION. Justification is a one-time act that frees a sinner from the guilt of sin at the time of conversion. Sanctification is a process by which God removes the pollution of sin. This process of progressive sanctification involves continual cooperation with the Holy Spirit. The Reformed approach to sanctification doesn't include a second spiritual experience. Rather, the Christian life is a day-by-day struggle with sin. Believers should expect victory over sin, but it won't come in a way that immediately brings success. Nearly always the classic Reformed writers confessed having days of prayer and agonizing with God to find the peace of victory. The more believers know Christ, the more they have an awareness of sin. Struggling with sin is quite compatible with progress toward purity.

THE REFORMED TRADITION AFFIRMS THE ROLE OF THE HOLY SPIRIT IN BELIEVERS' LIVES. Reformed theologians consistently point out that the Holy Spirit brings the power to overcome sin. The basic Christian responsibility is to cooperate with the work of the Holy Spirit as He enables progress.

REFORMED THEOLOGIANS DISAGREE ON THE DEFINITION OF THE NEW NATURE. Theologians have long debated whether the old nature continues in the life of a believer. Augustine and Calvin held to the position that believers have two natures within that war with each other. More recent theologians in this tradition hold to the position that believers have only one nature—new life in Christ. The two-nature approach takes the position that the Holy Spirit progressively enables the new nature to dominate the old. The one-nature approach takes the position that the believer's life is progressively transformed into a lifestyle consistent with the new nature given at conversion.

THE REFORMED TRADITION BELIEVES CHRISTIANS WILL CONTINUE TO SIN UNTIL DEATH. Christians won't be able to completely overcome sin and display lives of purity on the earth. They'll always struggle with sin until they reach the deliverance that comes when they see Christ. In the meantime, the Holy Spirit brings power to overcome and experience holiness.

Go back and underline the Reformed beliefs you agree with.

Which approach to sanctification do you most closely agree with? Why?

Christians differ on the specifics of how to become holy and even on the terms used to describe a life of holiness. Yet we find unity in one major concern. All agree that Christians should live holy lives that display the purity of Christian character. Only holiness pleases God and truly represents Christ to the world around us.

Spend time in prayer thanking God for making possible a life of holiness that culminates with complete holiness in His presence. Ask Him to work through His Spirit to guide, teach, and empower you in this process. Yield your heart to His work in your life.

1. David Peterson makes a valid distinction between sanctification and holiness. In general, he uses the terms as follows. Sanctification is what God does for us at conversion; holiness is our responsibility to live out the implications of sanctification. Although his point is helpful, it seems the Bible uses *sanctification* in present terms as an incentive to overcome sin (see 1 Thess. 4:3-6). Further, the distinction is largely based on the English translations of the Greek words for *sanctification* and *holiness*. Completely maintaining the distinction seems unsupportable in some contexts where the textual environment supports the present use. Nevertheless, David Peterson's book is of great value, and I'm in basic agreement with it. See David Peterson, *Possessed by God: A New Testament Theology of Sanctification and Holiness* (Grand Rapids, MI: William B. Eerdmans, 1995), 12–14.
2. There are many helpful references for understanding the positions that will be briefly described. Some of the most helpful because of brevity, accuracy, and interaction among advocates of various positions are: Melvin E. Dieter, Anthony A. Hoekema, Stanley M. Horton, J. Robertson McQuilkin, and John F. Walvoord, *Five Views on Sanctification* (Grand Rapids, MI: Zondervan, 1987); Bruce Demarest, "Transformed into His Likeness," in *The Cross and Salvation* (Wheaton, IL: Crossway, 1997), 385–429; D. L. Alexander, ed., *Christian Spirituality: Five Views of Sanctification* (Downers Grove, IL: InterVarsity, 1988); and standard theology textbooks.
3. Demarest, *The Cross and Salvation,* 391.

CHAPTER 2 GROUP EXPERIENCE
THE MEANING OF HOLINESS

COMING TOGETHER

1. *Identify someone you would identify as holy. What qualities and actions characterize his or her life?*

2. *Are some Christians more holy than others? Why or why not?*

THE DIMENSIONS OF HOLINESS: IMMEDIATE POSITIONAL HOLINESS

1. *What does positional holiness mean? How does it occur?*

2. *Read Romans 6:3-5.*

Are you unaware that all of us who were baptized into Christ Jesus were baptized into His death? Therefore we were buried with Him by baptism into death, in order that, just as Christ was raised from the dead by the glory of the Father, so we too may walk in a new way of life. For if we have been joined with Him in the likeness of His death, we will certainly also be in the likeness of His resurrection.

How does your identification with Jesus' death and resurrection bring about positional holiness?

3. *Read Romans 4:6-8.*

David also speaks of the blessing of the man God credits righteousness to apart from works:
> How joyful are those whose lawless acts are
> forgiven and whose sins are covered!
> How joyful is the man the Lord will never charge with sin!

How does our salvation experience change the way God sees us?

4. *In 1 Corinthians 1:2 Paul addressed his readers as "sanctified in Christ Jesus and called to be holy" (NIV). Yet his letter reveals that the church had many problems with sin. Why did Paul address the church this way? How can Christians be described as sinful and holy at the same time?*

5. *Read Ephesians 2:4-7.*

God, who is rich in mercy, because of His great love that He had for us, made us alive with the Messiah even though we were dead in trespasses. You are saved by grace! Together with Christ Jesus He also raised us up and seated us in the heavens, so that in the coming ages He might display the immeasurable riches of His grace through His kindness to us in Christ Jesus.

How do these verses give hope to believers who don't feel holy?

6. *How does an understanding of positional holiness change the way you see yourself?*

THE DIMENSIONS OF HOLINESS: CONTINUING PROGRESSIVE HOLINESS

1. *Read the following verses.*

Do not let sin reign in your mortal body so that you obey its desires. And do not offer any parts of it to sin as weapons for unrighteousness. But as those who are alive from the dead, offer yourselves to God, and all the parts of yourselves to God as weapons for righteousness.

ROMANS 6:12-13

Holy brothers, who share in the heavenly calling, fix your thoughts on Jesus, the apostle and high priest whom we confess.

HEBREWS 3:1, NIV

Submit to God. But resist the Devil, and he will flee from you. Draw near to God, and He will draw near to you. Cleanse your hands, sinners, and purify your hearts, double-minded people! Be miserable and mourn and weep. Your laughter must change to mourning and your joy to sorrow. Humble yourselves before the Lord, and He will exalt you.

JAMES 4:7-10

Prepare your minds for action; be self-controlled; set your hope fully on the grace to be given you when Jesus Christ is revealed. As obedient children, do not conform to the evil desires you had when you lived in ignorance.

1 PETER 1:13-14, NIV

How can these commands help us grow in holiness?

THE DIMENSIONS OF HOLINESS: ULTIMATE COMPLETE HOLINESS

1. Can believers attain complete holiness on earth? Why or why not?

2. How does the prospect of ultimate holiness affect your Christian walk on earth?

CONTEMPORARY EVANGELICAL
APPROACHES TO SANCTIFICATION

1. *Discuss highlights of the following approaches to sanctification, presented in chapter 2. With which positions do you agree or disagree?*

   • *Wesleyan*

   • *Pentecostal*

   • *Keswick*

   • *Reformed*

2. *How would you characterize the sanctification process in your life?*

3. *Why do you think many Christians fail to grow in the image of Christ?*

4. *Pray and thank God for the process of sanctification, which will lead to complete holiness in His presence. Ask Him to progressively make you more holy and Christlike as you yield to His sanctifying work in your life.*

PERSONAL TRANSFORMATION

CHAPTER 3
WHO AM I?

Christians ought to be different. Whether we like it or not, we have a responsibility to live a changed life when we profess Christ. People expect Christians never to lose their temper, become impatient, curse, gossip, complain, or do anything else wrong. The common expectation is that on conversion to Christ, we adopted a new way of living.

As Christians, we react to this expectation. We realize though redeemed, we still have a strong tendency to sin. We know our inner struggles. Further, we know temptations to sin grow stronger once we identify with Christ. At times we wish unbelievers understood those dynamics and had more sympathy for our challenges. The fact is they don't.

An even more important issue than the way others perceive us is the expectation to live by biblical teachings. If we're seeking permission to live a sinful life, we won't find it in the Bible. The standards in God's Word are high. God expects His people to be holy, set apart to Him and from the world. He expects us to replace the patterns of the pre-Christian life with new values, priorities, and lifestyles.

What new expectations did you notice after you accepted Christ?

How did you respond to those new expectations?

We find a constant tension in our lives. On the one hand, we desire to be like Christ. We recognize the sinful disposition that characterized us before conversion, and we want to be as holy and pure as possible. On the other hand, we have constant battles with sin. Although we have new life in Christ, we still struggle with sin, and we often fail. In this chapter we will focus on the believer's ongoing battle with sin.

If we're going to grow in holiness, we need to understand what holiness looks like. At the same time, we need to avoid a list approach to godly living, because any list of holy behaviors can change from place to place and time to time. In contrast, basic principles of holiness transcend time and place. Not all Christians grasp these basic principles, so they fail to grow spiritually and fall short of the joy of holy living.

Being set apart for God means living according to His plan, based on His holy character. It's living by God's economy rather than our own. The more we're able to live out our conversion experience in life, the more we'll be fulfilled and at peace. The principles of the Christian life presented in this chapter aren't add-ons to conversion. They aren't optional. They come at conversion with regeneration, and God expects us to grow consistently from that point forward.

In the previous chapter I mentioned the concern some people express about terminology related to holiness. I stated that I use the terms *holiness* and *sanctification* synonymously. I take the position that transformation is very much a part of holiness, or sanctification.

Because God begins His work of sanctification in our minds, we can't grow in Christlikeness without understanding who we are as believers. But this understanding alone won't bring victory over sin or the holiness we desire. A change of life involves a change of self-identity. That means if we want to live a holy life, we must start by understanding who we really are as believers.

> *Recall a time when you struggled with a temptation to sin. Now recall an occasion when you obeyed God. Consider how your thoughts and feelings differed. How did you grow from these experiences?*

FROM THE OLD TO THE NEW

The Bible uses several terms to describe a Christian's experience as new. Perhaps the most clearly stated is 2 Corinthians 5:

> If anyone is in Christ, he is a new creation;
> old things have passed away, and look, new things have come.

2 CORINTHIANS 5:17

Most people understand this verse to mean that when a person accepts Christ, a new life begins. Recently, many scholars have interpreted it to express Paul's hope that a new age has come. According to this view, Paul stated that at his conversion he entered the new age ushered in by Jesus' death and resurrection. Both interpretations stress the fact that something new happens to a believer. What is that newness?

Paul described in three Scriptures the change that occurs in believers as they move from the old to the new:

> We know that our old self was crucified with Him in order
> that sin's dominion over the body may be abolished,
> so that we may no longer be enslaved to sin.
>
> **ROMANS 6:6**

> You took off your former way of life, the old self
> that is corrupted by deceitful desires.
>
> **EPHESIANS 4:22**

> Do not lie to one another, since you have put off the old self
> with its practices and have put on the new self. You are being
> renewed in knowledge according to the image of your Creator.
>
> **COLOSSIANS 3:9-10**

What stands out most to you in these passages?

What do they teach about the old self?

The Greek word translated *old self* is *anthropos,* a general word often meaning *humanity,* which includes both man and woman. Most translations use the terms *old self* and *new self* to express the idea of a believer's transformation from the old nature to the new nature. What did Paul mean by *old self* and *new self*?

The most instructive passage in this group is Colossians 3:9-10. It parallels Ephesians 4:22 and complements Romans 6:6. In this section of Colossians, Paul explained how to live consistently after conversion. He described who Jesus is (see 1:9-23) and what Jesus' death means to those who follow Christ (see 2:6–3:4). Paul then turned to practical implications of the Christian life, including practical holiness.

Christians are to "put to death what belongs to your worldly nature" (3:5). These things are explained in two groups of five—one personal and one social. The personal concerns are "sexual immorality, impurity, lust, evil desire, and greed, which is idolatry" (v. 5). The social concerns are "anger, wrath, malice, slander, and filthy language" (v. 8). A final admonition addresses lying. Christians are not to "lie to one another" (v. 9). Lying has no place in God's economy.

Paul gave a reason to turn away from the characteristics of the old life:

> … since you have put off the old self with its practices
> and have put on the new self. You are being renewed in
> knowledge according to the image of your Creator.
>
> **COLOSSIANS 3:9-10**

These verses indicate a decisive change. The command to "put to death" (v. 5) is impossible without this change. Two important points emerge.

1. Paul based his commands for holy living on the conversion experience. He didn't tell his readers to die to self. That occurred when they chose to identify with Christ and His death (see Rom. 6:1-4). Furthermore, Paul never used the phrase *die to self* as an explanation of how to live the Christian life. When he used the metaphor of death, it was to end the activities that characterize the former life.

2. It appears that the church in Colosse hadn't attained holiness. If the believers had been holy, Paul's commands would have had no relevance. Nevertheless, they'd been changed, whether or not the new self appeared as the dominant characteristic of their lives. Converted people may still be quite sinful in their actions even though they've experienced salvation.

Both of these points help us understand that death to self is a past experience for believers.

How would you describe what it means to put to death the old self?

How would you describe your struggle with sin even after conversion?

Colossians 3:9-10 also reveals that the past experience of death to self leads to an ongoing change in life toward Christlikeness. The need to grow is further emphasized by verse 10, in which Paul explained that the new self is "being renewed in knowledge according to the image of your Creator." Even the new self can't claim perfection. Rather, it must constantly be transformed to become holy. The goal—being like the Creator—is the end of a process that starts at conversion and continues with ever-increasing knowledge that leads to obedience. The Colossians were in process, just as we are.

What progress have you seen in growing toward Christlikeness since you were saved?

From this passage we can glean the logical sequence of events in conversion.

1. Taking off the old self

2. Putting on the new self

3. Being renewed in knowledge of the Creator

From the language used here, it appears that the old self and new self are incompatible. That is, they don't coexist. Otherwise, putting off and putting on make no sense. Further, the transactions of putting off and putting on don't preclude the necessity of growth. Thus, a twofold dynamic is at work. One is conversion, when the old person is put off. The other is the ongoing transformation of life that takes place through the knowledge of Christ.

In the parallel passage, Ephesians 4, Paul contrasted the life of the Gentiles with the life of Christians. Paul identified the Gentiles here because they represented the way godless people live. After describing a lifestyle of immorality and insensitivity to God, Paul complimented the church for the change of behavior that occurred at conversion. In Ephesians 4:20 he stated, "You, however, did not come to know Christ that way" (NIV). He mentally took them back to their conversion experience. At the time of their conversion, they knew better than to continue living as the Gentiles lived. Paul made this point explicit in verses 22-24:

You were taught, with regard to your former way of life, to put off your old self, which is being corrupted by its deceitful desires; to be made new in the attitude of your minds; and to put on the new self, created to be like God in true righteousness and holiness.

EPHESIANS 4:22-24 (NIV)

The primary difference between this passage and the one in Colossians is the sequence of events. In Ephesians Paul stressed the truth that growth in knowledge was a part of salvation. More precisely, he used the word *attitude* rather than *knowledge* (Greek, *noos).* At conversion the Ephesians had a change of attitude about the old person and the new person. This change of attitude led them to embrace the values of the new person.

Something new happened at conversion. Although some read the words *to put off* as future and therefore relevant to a Christian's postconversion life, in actuality the context reveals that Paul used the words in the past tense. The entire context speaks of knowledge that enabled the Ephesians to come to a point of salvation. Further, as in Colossians, there's an antithesis between the old self and the new self. They don't coexist.

The third passage employing the old-person terminology is Romans 6. In verse 6 Paul stated, "We know that our old self was crucified with him." Once again, the verbs are in the past tense, describing something that happened at conversion. The point of Romans 6:1-14 is to help the new self live consistently in light of the conversion experience. Again, the passage reveals that the old self and the new self don't coexist: "Consider yourselves dead to sin but alive to God in Christ Jesus" (v. 11).

How is a Christian's life different from an unbeliever's life in regard to—

identity?

sin?

holiness?

purpose?

So the three passages we've studied describe the change from the old person to the new person as taking place at conversion, and the two selves don't coexist.

This discussion leads to an important question: Who are the old person and the new person anyway? The old-person question has been answered from several perspectives, based on Paul's teachings.

THEOLOGICALLY. Those who take a theological approach often equate the old person with the positional truth that the old life is past.

PSYCHOLOGICALLY. Viewed from this perspective, the old person is a nature. The Bible uses the word *nature* to explain why unbelievers act as they do (see Eph. 2:3), but such uses are rare. There's little to suggest that the old person and nature are to be equated.

PHILOSOPHICALLY. Some people equate the term *old person* with the substance of human beings. They often argue that something real—the substance of our beings— changes at conversion.

HISTORICALLY. In this approach the old person refers to a period of time or, better, a situation in a believer's life. Those who understand the phrase this way point out the historical sequences of movement from one situation called unbelief to another called faith.

ESCHATOLOGICALLY. Proponents of this view teach that the terms *old nature* and *new nature* are corporate. The old person is the present evil age, while the new person is the age of salvation ushered in by Jesus Christ. This final position interprets all the previous texts corporately rather than individually, so individuals find themselves in the new age because of Christ. As part of that new age, individual believers should live pure lives.

Based on the Scriptures you've read so far in this chapter, what do you think Paul meant by—

the old nature?

the new nature?

THE STRUGGLE TO CHANGE

So far our consideration of the old person and the new person hasn't addressed this core issue: What actually changes about people when they're redeemed?

What's your response to that question?

The old person has a characteristic way of doing things. Because he's blinded by sin and motivated by self-interests, every action revolves around self and is sinful. The old person embodies the way a believer lived before salvation.

Basically, all of life before Christ is blinded by darkness and soiled by sin. This doesn't mean a non-Christian is incapable of doing good things. The image of God in us motivates us to good actions, both individually and socially. Paul explained this in Romans 2. He discussed the possibility that people who don't know God's will (the law) can actually do things commanded in the law:

When Gentiles, who do not have the law, instinctively do what the law demands, they are a law to themselves even though they do not have the law. They show that the work of the law is written on their hearts. Their consciences confirm this.

ROMANS 2:14-15

Do you think a lost person is capable of doing good? Why or why not?

On the other hand, at conversion things change. New life is far more complex than the old life. We have times of victory, times of defeat, and times of ambivalence. Even so, in the core of our being, we desire to know God and to be like Him because of His work of regeneration in our hearts.

The new person is all someone is and can be. This new person has new motivations, new ambitions, new attitudes, new actions, and new patterns for relationships. At conversion God changes the old motivations for action to new ones. Believers seek God. They value His will, and they have an innate desire for holiness. Although this desire can be distorted and diminished by sin, it can't be eradicated. This truth explains why Christians are often frustrated by their own thoughts and behaviors.

In spite of being new persons, Christians struggle with sin. That doesn't mean they struggle with the question of whether they *want* to sin. That question was settled at conversion. Christians don't want to sin, but their inner struggle may continue to bring tension to their daily walk with the Lord.

Read about Paul's struggles with sin in Romans 7:14-25. How is sin causing struggles and frustrations in your Christian life?

What evidence in your life shows that you want to know and obey God in spite of your struggles with sin?

The struggle is often intense. Paul presented the struggle from two different perspectives—the law and his own nature. But he never described the struggle as being waged between two natures. Rather, the problem was a struggle between what he knew he should do and the flesh that wouldn't do it:

> I do not understand what I am doing, because I do not
> practice what I want to do, but I do what I hate.
>
> **ROMANS 7:15**

Paul also described this struggle in Galatians as a conflict between the Spirit and the flesh:

> I say then, walk by the Spirit and you will not carry out the
> desire of the flesh. For the flesh desires what is against the
> Spirit, and the Spirit desires what is against the flesh; these are
> opposed to each other, so that you don't do what you want.
> But if you are led by the Spirit, you are not under the law.
>
> **GALATIANS 5:16-18**

We should note two points about these texts.

1. The two passages teach nothing about two natures. The struggle consists of the failure to accomplish the transformation the mind desires. In spite of that, we struggle to become better.

2. The struggle indicates a frustration factor. Frustration comes from the inability to live up to the knowledge we possess. These passages explain a basic component of the Christian life. When we fail to live up to what we know to do, we're frustrated. When our lives fail to conform to the insights of the mind, we'll experience frustration.

The solution is Jesus Christ. He alone brings desire and performance into harmony. After describing his frustration with the flesh, Paul wrote:

What a wretched man I am! Who will rescue me from this dying body? I thank God through Jesus Christ our Lord!

ROMANS 7:24-25

On the other hand, when we live up to God's expectations for new life in Christ, we experience peace. But without His help, none of us can bring our lives in line with His expectations.

What are some ways you seek God's help in overcoming sin and conforming to His expectations for a holy life?

The issues raised in our discussion of the new nature can be illustrated by the different phases of a man's life. When men aren't married, we call them bachelors. When a bachelor chooses a woman to be his wife, there's usually an engagement period. During that time he's still a bachelor, but even then there are indications that his life's about to change—radically. During the wedding the bachelor promises himself to the woman, and the pastor pronounces the couple husband and wife. In an instant the man's situation is changed. He's no longer a bachelor; he's a husband.

In his vows the man promises to be a husband, and both he and his wife hope he will be a good one. Still, sometimes problems arise in a relationship. Some husbands never quite grasp the concept, continuing to live as if their own interests and needs are primary. Perhaps they continue going out with the guys. Perhaps they spend all their money on themselves. Some even run around with other women, disregarding their vows of purity and monogamy. People may react by asking, "Doesn't he know he has a wife?" "Doesn't he know he made promises?" "Doesn't he know he's no longer a bachelor?"

This last question targets the problem. Regardless of how the husband lives after his marriage, he's no longer a bachelor. The solution is to realize and accept who he really is—a husband—and live out his commitment to married life. Further, the more he fails to act like a husband, the more frustrated he will become. Everywhere he goes and no matter what he does, a voice inside reminds him that he's not keeping the commitment he made. In other words, a married man can't act like a bachelor and be happy about it.

When individuals come to Christ, the experience is similar to a wedding. In a single moment promises are made that affect them for the rest of their lives. Once Christians are converted, they become new persons. No matter what they do or how they live, they'll always be the new person. When a Christian disobeys Christ, it's similar to the husband who continues to live like a bachelor. The relationship with Christ is affected when Christians live disobedient lives. Even though their hearts may be deeply committed to the things of God, they won't experience the joy of salvation, and they'll carry guilt and frustration into every aspect of their lives. Failure to achieve victory over sin is the result of living inappropriately. Christians can't respond to their own sin by saying, "That was my old person."

THE ONE-NATURE APPROACH

Over the centuries theologians have debated the implications of Paul's teachings on the old self and the new self. Most of the discussion about sanctification revolves around the following two questions.

1. Are there two natures within a believer, and if so, what are they?

2. If there is only one nature, how do we explain Paul's terminology?

Basically, proponents of a one-nature view believe at conversion the old nature is replaced by the new nature. Those who advance a two-nature approach believe the new nature resides alongside the old nature, and the two natures continually war with each other.

We'll begin by examining the one-nature view of humanity. Proponents of this position contend that unbelievers have only one nature. It's a disposition that embraces sin and actions that are contrary to God. It's the residue of Adam's sin passed down to all people. At conversion the old nature is changed so that it embraces God. Still, learning new life patterns takes time, so change comes progressively throughout the believer's new life. Even so, God implants a deep desire to be obedient and to follow a life of holiness, enabling such a life through the work of the Holy Spirit.

The central issue in this approach is, Why do we sin? Those who hold to one nature explain that a believer's nature progressively changes. Conversion doesn't mean the believer can't sin. It only means the believer no longer *wants* to sin. The Holy Spirit brings the power to change the believer's nature. As the believer cooperates with the work of the Spirit, the believer's nature is changed into the purity God expects. Therefore, our one nature— the only nature we'll ever have—is transformed toward holiness.

What strengths do you see in the one-nature approach?

What questions does it raise?

If people have one nature, what does the Bible teach about that nature? We'll overview the three primary stages of human development—preconversion, postconversion, and the eternal state—to summarize a biblical view of the one-nature approach.

PRECONVERSION. The preconversion situation is clear. Many New Testament passages speak of the unbeliever as limited by the Adam-only existence (see Rom. 5:12-21). In Adam the entire person has a disposition to sin. Indeed, everything an unbeliever does is touched by sin and is usually evidenced by a central egocentricity that understands the world as revolving around the individual and his or her interests.

The blinding effects of sin keep us from understanding what God really expects from us. Theologians call this the noetic effects of sin, "ways that sin negatively affects and undermines the human mind and intellect."[1] Passages such as Romans 1:18–3:20 (especially 3:9-20); 5:12-21; and Ephesians 2:1-3,11-13 clearly express the effects of sin. Often the biblical writers describe that state as "in Adam" (1 Cor. 15:22), "the old self" (Rom. 6:6; Eph. 4:22; Col. 3:9), and "the flesh" (Rom. 8 and others). Without a doubt, the preconversion person can be described as having a sin nature.

What were some of the blinding effects of sin in your life before you became a believer?

POSTCONVERSION. The postconversion situation receives the most discussion in the Bible. Conversion brings an immediate change that leads to an ongoing, progressive change of behavior as a person puts off the old person and puts on the new (see Rom. 6:6; Eph. 4:22-24; Col. 3:9-10). Ephesians uses the words "took off" the old (v. 22). Colossians states it as "put off" (v. 9), while Romans 6:6 uses the word "crucified." All speak to a separation from the past. The believer is no longer bound by the patterns of the past. The guilt of sin is removed, and the believer has new motivations, goals, and ambitions. Paul himself is a prime example of someone who put off the old self when he was converted.

What immediate changes did conversion bring in your life?

A progressive change of behavior comes as the believer acts in accord with salvation. The passages that speak of putting off the old person also speak of the need to conquer the sinful acts that characterized the past. Paul described the believer's responsibility this way: "Put to death what belongs to your worldly nature" (Col. 3:5).

This instruction has been variously explained in history. Some have taken it almost literally, thinking the best form of holiness was achieved by physical abuse of the body. But Paul didn't decry physical comfort or health; they aren't the basic enemies of holiness. Others have understood this instruction to mean that believers are to put our personhood to death. These people reject personality, ambition, energy, and anything else that brings the personal satisfaction of achievement. They say anything that allows the physical body and identity to be prominent is contrary to God's will. Death, after all, means nonexistence.

A better understanding of Colossians 3:5 is that Paul wrote figuratively. The language is strong but appropriate, indicating that the activities identified aren't to predominate as they did before. Passages like these state that believers are to do whatever possible to remove any trace of these sins in their lives.

Paul said to put to death "what belongs to your worldly nature." The Greek is literally *members*. Normally, the Greek word *mele* referred to bodily parts. Paul frequently used it to refer to activities promoted by the physical body:

> Put to death what belongs to your worldly nature: sexual immorality, impurity, lust, evil desire, and greed, which is idolatry, ... anger, wrath, malice, slander, and filthy language from your mouth.

COLOSSIANS 3:5-8

Paul suggested that the body promoted these activities in the past. The old person did these things because of who he was and how he used his parts (members).

At conversion things change. The old person no longer exists, so the activities associated with his way of doing things should cease. We're to cease the old person's way of doing things by a conscious choice on our part and with the divine help of the Holy Spirit.

Describe one way the Holy Spirit helped you put away a sinful action after you were saved.

Ephesians 4:22-24 addresses the same issues, even though the context reveals the issues are to be understood in relationship to the church. There's a corporate focus. Even so, the group can't progress as it should unless individual believers grow in holiness. Ephesians 4 contrasts the preconversion experience (see vv. 17-19) with postconversion expectations (see 4:20–6:20). Because the Ephesian believers learned to take off "the old self" (4:22) and to "put on the new" (4:24), they should devote themselves to stopping preconversion sinful activities and to promoting attitudes that encourage new life in Christ.

In Romans 6:1-14 Paul addressed the necessity of life transformation after conversion. All Christians should apply the meaning of the cross to their own lives. Christians identify with Christ in death and resurrection (see vv. 1-5). This means at conversion we "died with Christ" (v. 8) and were enabled to live a new life. The sequence of thought involves a purpose, an illustration, and some commands for the believer.

Read Romans 6:4. How does our identification with Christ enable us to overcome sin?

The purpose of our identification with Christ in death and resurrection is to overcome sin, as taught in Romans 6:6. Three phrases occur sequentially, and each one depends on the phrase that preceded it. Paul started with "Our old self was crucified with Him." He continued with "in order that sin's dominion over the body may be abolished." There's less unanimity on the meaning of this phrase. Many understand it as synonymous with the old self's being crucified. But the Greek language doesn't comfortably allow that interpretation. It signifies the direct purpose of the crucifixion of the old self. Some have taken this phrase to mean that the physical body should be eliminated. Stopping short of death, they've mutilated and buffeted their bodies into conformity. Others have understood the body of sin as the mass of sin, that is, sin in its entirety.

It's best to understand the body of sin as the body characterized by sin. This interpretation fits the injunctions of Colossians 3:5, where Paul taught that the old person's crucifixion should lead to ceasing the use of our bodies for sin and its purposes:

> Put to death what belongs to your worldly nature: sexual immorality, impurity, lust, evil desire and greed, which is idolatry.
>
> **COLOSSIANS 3:5**

The ultimate goal is that "we may no longer be enslaved to sin" (Rom. 6:6). *Slavery* means *complete obedience out of obligation.* When sin is the master, as it is for all people born into this world, it demands complete obedience. But the crucifixion of the old person should lead to a new freedom to act in accord with God's will so that sin's dominance is broken.

An illustration of a believer's death to sin draws on the analogy already presented. The believer has died, been buried, and been raised with Christ (see 6:1-3). Such a death is a one-time experience (see 6:9), both for Christ and for the believer. After death the believer enters a resurrection life that lasts forever without the interruption brought by death. Jesus "died to sin" (6:10), and the believer died in the same way.

The illustration draws a parallel that helps us understand the nature of the death-to-sin experience at conversion. Jesus voluntarily died to sin, putting Himself under sin to defeat sin in death. An unbeliever lives under sin but, unlike Christ, is dominated and influenced by it. But because Christ triumphed over sin and death, He enables those who believe in Him to die to sin also. When He died, we died with Him. His death to sin empowers us to die to sin as well.

What's your response to the teaching in Romans 6 that you died with Christ?

This is a judicial description. It's a reality that occurs spiritually now, to be completed at the time of the resurrection from the dead. Nevertheless, our identification with Christ brings power in this life not only for salvation but also for future spiritual transformation. At our conversion God breathes into our old self the breath of new life and enables the new self to thrive. The passages we've studied in relation to our postconversion state not only describe immediate changes at conversion but also progressive changes through the process of sanctification.

Explain why you believe as a Christian, you're no longer a slave to sin.

If believers have a new nature that's no longer a slave to sin, why do we continue to sin?

THE ETERNAL STATE. Having passed through the preconversion and postconversion states, we enter the eternal state. The entrance into the eternal state has two phases.

1. When believers die, they immediately enter heaven to be with Christ. This is a full state of consciousness, and it includes all of a person's nonphysical aspects.

2. The second phase occurs at the resurrection. The resurrection of the dead occurs at the second coming of Christ. Until that time the body remains on earth or in the grave (see 1 Cor. 15:35-58; 1 Thess. 4:13-18). When Jesus comes, the struggle with sin will be over, and Christians will live in complete holiness with Christ forever.

Biblical teachings clearly demonstrate a one-nature view of humanity.

Do you agree with the assertion that the Bible clearly supports a one-nature view of humanity? Why or why not?

THE TWO-NATURE APPROACH

A significant number of people teach that both the old self and the new self are present in believers. Those who hold the position that a believer has two natures follow the teachings of the early church fathers, with Augustine usually credited with developing the idea. There are some variations, but the basic idea is as follows. The two natures within believers correspond to the two experiences of Christians. The believer used to be in an unregenerate state, described as "in Adam," "in the flesh," or the "old self." The first nature, therefore, comes from Adam and is passed through birth to every person. That nature is characterized by self-orientation and a strong love for sin. Decidedly anti-God and contrary to His purposes, it characterizes every non-Christian. At conversion the believer in Christ receives a new nature. Corresponding to the new life at conversion, this new nature comes from Christ. It's characterized by a God-orientation and a desire to be submissive to Christ. It loves holiness and purity.

Only Christians possess the new nature. Yet Christians also possess the old nature. This means in every believer there remains a love for and tendency toward sin. The old nature explains believers' constant struggle with sin and their sensitivity to temptation. At the same time, believers have a hatred for sin and a love of God because of their new nature. Having both of these natures means there's a constant battle between them. Because of the intensity of the battle, we need an arbitrator who determines what the person actually does. That arbitrator is the Holy Spirit. The Spirit fights against the old nature so that the new nature can dominate. Believers who allow the Holy Spirit to control their lives display the work of the Spirit.

What strengths do you see in the two-nature approach?

What questions does it raise?

Those who hold to a two-nature approach draw their position from two sources: Scripture and the Christian experience.

SCRIPTURE. Multiple Scripture passages are interpreted to explain the continuing spiritual battle in the lives of Christians. Paul said, for example, that we must put to death our members and activities that are vehicles for sin:

> Each of you must put off falsehood and speak truthfully
> to his neighbor, for we are all members of one body.
> **EPHESIANS 4:25, NIV**

> Put to death what belongs to your worldly nature: sexual immorality,
> impurity, lust, evil desire, and greed, which is idolatry.
> **COLOSSIANS 3:5**

The two-nature approach to interpreting these passages indicate that even though we've put off the old person and put on the new, we must continually reinforce that action by putting off the activities of the old person and putting on the new activities. The command to put to death the deeds of the flesh implies the need to complete something that's already accomplished.

What's already been accomplished in putting off your old self?

What remains to be accomplished in putting on your new self?

CHRISTIAN EXPERIENCE. Those who argue for the presence of two natures in a believer also point out experiential characteristics. All believers struggle with an inward pull toward sin. How are we to explain the tendency to sin if the old person is no longer resident within? The experiential argument provides a powerful explanation for the fact that believers continue to sin. After all, the tendency to sin originated in the old person.

Neither of these arguments explains Scripture well. As for the biblical basis for the two-nature explanation, the language of the Bible clearly distinguishes between the change at conversion and the changes expected as a result of conversion. The *death* terminology generally applies to learning to live after conversion. Christians put to death certain sinful activities and attitudes. In other words, our lives should conform to what's actually happened to us when we were saved. This language perfectly fits with the tension we've already seen between sanctification as positional and sanctification as progressive.

The experiential argument for the two-nature theory also calls for careful thought. It's true that even Christians sin. Because such sinful acts and attitudes are identified with the old person, it stands to reason that some think the old person still lives in a believer. However, such reasoning doesn't fit the language of Scripture. In fact, Scripture teaches that the reason to put to death sinfully motivated acts is that they're inconsistent with who we really are. We really are the new person. The new person shouldn't act like the old person.

PROBLEMS WITH THE TWO-NATURE APPROACH

Many Christians hold to some form of the two-nature position. Nevertheless, it seems that Scripture teaches a unified nature of all people, including believers. Accepting a two-nature approach to the essence of Christians raises basic problems that are biblical, soteriological (relating to the theology of salvation), psychological, and eschatological (relating to the theology of end times).

BIBLICAL ISSUES

The Bible never uses the word *nature* in describing two different motivations toward life. In Ephesians 2:3 Paul spoke of the Gentiles who do sinful acts "by nature". He also attributed immorality and idolatry to a natural state of unbelievers. However, the Bible never talks about a new nature being given to anyone. The only use of the term *nature* in relation to believers occurs in 2 Peter 1:4:

> By these He has given us very great and precious promises,
> so that through them you may share in the divine nature escaping
> the corruption that is in the world because of evil desires.
>
> **2 PETER 1:4**

This text probably has a future reference consistent with its context. It teaches that God has given us great promises that will empower us to escape the corruption of the world someday and to share in the divine nature. Verses 5-9 exhort believers to develop Christian virtues as the most certain protection from being entrapped in the corruption of the world. Thus, Scripture's clear testimony speaks of only one nature when the word *nature* is used.

SOTERIOLOGICAL ISSUES

The two-nature theory also raises questions about the nature of regeneration. Orthodox Christians have always affirmed the fact that at conversion an unbeliever is regenerated. Substantial discussion relates to the issue of what's regenerated. For our purposes here the question must be asked of the human nature. Is it regenerated? Rather than affirming a substantive change in a person at conversion, the two-nature approach simply states that at conversion God gives a new nature. The position basically affirms that God adds to the person rather than transforming what already exists. That raises serious questions about what's changed in the old person.

Biblical teachings on salvation lend credence to the one-nature position on sanctification. *Regeneration* comes from words that mean *to be born again.* The opening of eyes to spiritual sight is a change in the unbeliever. It's a work of the Holy Spirit enabling the old person to respond to the Spirit in repentance and faith, thereby becoming a new person.

In the two-nature approach a new nature is given to the believer, and this new nature coexists with the already present old nature. We have to question whether a two-nature view is true to the doctrine of regeneration. To say that regeneration simply brings the new nature is to imply that God somehow implants the new nature without regard to the old. Such an argument doesn't conform to Scripture. Instead, the Bible indicates that the old self is renewed and regenerated, and that enables the new self to replace the old.

PSYCHOLOGICAL ISSUES

Accepting the two-nature theory also raises questions about Christian victory. If the two natures war against each other at every decisive point of temptation, then who determines which nature wins, and how does that nature win? The two-nature theory leaves the person as a neutral observer of two powers or at least inner influences. The believer is passive and neutral, a nonparticipant in the battle but very much affected by the strength of both natures.

In Scripture Christians are never encouraged to be passive about the Christian life. Some suggest that one nature defeats the other because of the choices we make. That is, if a Christian chooses the old nature's actions, it wins, and vice versa. But what or who influences the choice? The response may well be that the Holy Spirit does. Even so, with this approach the person doesn't overcome; the nature does.

The one-nature view of sanctification clarifies the psychological issues raised by the two-nature position. This position doesn't suggest that the individual has power to effect the changes necessary for Christian growth, but it does mean that no growth occurs without a believer's conscious choice. The entire New Testament assumes that Christians are responsible for their growth in holiness. The old person becomes the new person as God begins His work of transformation at the person's conversion.

ESCHATOLOGICAL ISSUES

The two-nature approach raises questions about what's finally redeemed and transformed when a believer is called to heaven. Is part of the believer left behind—the old nature that never submitted to Christ? If this is the case, only a portion of the Christian would enter heaven and enjoy the blessings of salvation. The old nature, a continuing part of the person, would be left behind.

The one-nature position answers concerns about the nature of the resurrected person. Scripture teaches that the entire person—everything he or she is—will be carried to heaven. The assumption is that the new nature is completed at that time, and the old nature is completely gone. A basic theme of redemption is that God redeems every facet of creation touched by sin.

Are there facets of your life that aren't fit for heaven? How are you pursuing holiness as you deal with these issues in your life?

Only the one-nature view adequately explains the change you experience at conversion. At that time you're changed. You're regenerated. The old nature is gone. The new nature has come. Therefore, you're responsible for your life and your relationship with Christ. You can't blame failures on anyone else, including a bad nature. If all the proper ingredients are in place, in time you should mature and become a successful Christian, living up to your high calling in Jesus Christ. Chapter 4 will reveal the proper ingredients for growing toward holiness.

Mark the following scales to evaluate your attitude toward your new life in Christ.

1	2	3	4	5	6	7	8	9	10

Giving in to sin   *Seeking holiness*

1	2	3	4	5	6	7	8	9	10

Blaming my sins on others   *Accepting responsibility for sin and failure*

1	2	3	4	5	6	7	8	9	10

Continuing old behaviors   *Intentionally growing in Christ*

Express to God your desire to take off the old self and put on the new. Ask Him to show you specific attitudes and behaviors that need to change. Ask Him to give you wisdom, power, and perseverance to make those changes.

1."Noetic effects of sin" [online, cited 5 March 2014]. Available from the Internet: *www.theopedia.com.*

CHAPTER 3 GROUP EXPERIENCE
WHO AM I?

COMING TOGETHER

1. In what ways did you immediately change when you became a Christian?

2. How is your new identity different from your identity when you weren't a believer?

FROM THE OLD TO THE NEW

1. Read the following verses.

We know that our old self was crucified with Him in order
that sin's dominion over the body may be abolished,
so that we may no longer be enslaved to sin.

ROMANS 6:6

You were taught, with regard to your former way of life, to put off
your old self, which is being corrupted by its deceitful desires; to
be made new in the attitude of your minds; and to put on the new
self, created to be like God in true righteousness and holiness.

EPHESIANS 4:22-24, NIV

Do not lie to one another, since you have put off the old self
with its practices and have put on the new self. You are being
renewed in knowledge according to the image of your Creator.

COLOSSIANS 3:9-10

*What did Paul mean by the old self? What are some characteristics
of the old self?*

2. What did Paul mean by the new self? What are some characteristics of the new self?

3. Can the old self and the new self coexist? Why or why not?

THE STRUGGLE TO CHANGE

1. How is it possible for an unbeliever to do good things?

2. Why do believers continue to sin after conversion? Discuss and express agreement or disagreement with the author's explanation:

The central issue in [the one-nature] approach is, Why do we sin? Those who hold to one nature explain that a believer's nature progressively changes. Conversion doesn't mean the believer can't sin. It only means the believer no longer wants to sin. The Holy Spirit brings the power to change the believer's nature. As the believer cooperates with the work of the Spirit, the believer's nature is changed into the purity God expects. Therefore, our one nature—the only nature we'll ever have—is transformed toward holiness.

3. Read about Paul's struggles with sin in Romans 7:14-25. In what ways do you relate to Paul's struggles?

4. What help does God provide for Christians who want to overcome sin and grow in holiness?

THE ONE-NATURE APPROACH

1. Read the following verses.

Each of you must put off falsehood and speak truthfully to his neighbor, for we are all members of one body.

EPHESIANS 4:25, NIV

Put to death what belongs to your worldly nature: sexual immorality, impurity, lust, evil desire, and greed, which is idolatry.

COLOSSIANS 3:5

How would you describe the nature of someone before conversion?

2. How does a person's nature change when he or she is saved?

3. What did Paul mean when he wrote, "Put to death what belongs to your worldly nature" (Col. 3:5)?

4. How does conversion enable a believer to put sinful thoughts and behaviors to death?

5. How does the new nature set you on the path to growth in Christlikeness?

6. Read the following verse.

We were buried with Him by baptism into death, in order that, just as Christ was raised from the dead by the glory of the Father, so we too may walk in a new way of life.

ROMANS 6:4

How does identifying with Christ enable believers to overcome sin?

THE TWO-NATURE APPROACH

1. Read the following verses.

Each of you must put off falsehood and speak truthfully
to his neighbor, for we are all members of one body.

EPHESIANS 4:25, NIV

Put to death what belongs to your worldly nature: sexual immorality,
impurity, lust, evil desire, and greed, which is idolatry.

COLOSSIANS 3:5

*Some people believe Christians simultaneously possess two natures—
the old and the new. How can these passages be interpreted to support
that view?*

2. What evidence in human experience would support a two-nature view?

PROBLEMS WITH THE TWO-NATURE APPROACH

*1. What problems are raised by the idea that we possess two natures that
continually war with each other? How does the one-nature view counter
these issues?*

   • Biblical issues

   • Soteriological issues

   • Psychological issues

   • Eschatological issues

*2. Close by praying that God will empower you to put off the characteristics of
the old self and to put on the new as He renews you in the image of Christ.*

CHAPTER 4
WHAT'S NEW ABOUT A CHRISTIAN?

One day I had lunch with Gary, a very successful businessman. He'd been employed at the same major corporation since graduating from college approximately 25 years earlier. His compay had been good to him, and he exemplified the company's values. He rapidly advanced through the ranks, spending time in plants as well as in the main office. At this point Gary was working directly under the president.

However, Gary was having problems. Things at the office were pretty much the same, but Gary wasn't. In the middle of his career, he'd become a Christian. He rapidly grew in his faith and was delighted that his corporation operated from values consistent with his newfound faith.

Eventually, another corporate group with different values purchased Gary's company. He had increasing difficulty with the new corporate ethics and practices. Although the company affirmed him and advanced him beyond his peers, Gary was restless. His long hours affected his family. He found less time to be involved in church activities, and his energy was sapped. In addition, Gary didn't agree with some of the company's new contractual relationships. He felt increasing concern about promoting products in a politically repressive country.

Gary needed a change.

Many Christians experience similar challenges. Frequently, Christians' personal lives and corporate lives collide. Like Gary's work dilemma, their situations call for difficult decisions. On the one hand, a believer needs security, a good salary, and solid relationships. On the other, matters of conscience can relentlessly plague a believer's thoughts and dampen enthusiasm for all of life.

How have you experienced a conflict of values as a Christian?

Conversion brings conviction. The new person differs from the old person. Certainly the difference is felt, but what's actually different about a Christian? At least three areas of life reflect a change from the old to the new: values, ambitions, and pleasures.

VALUES OF THE CHRISTIAN LIFE

Values are the things we most prize—the things we hold most dear. Values motivate us to achieve. They also help us measure personal success. When we value health, we take care of our bodies. When we value family, we try to be our best for our spouses, children, and extended family. When we value God, we include Him in every aspect of our lives. Our values are foundational to life, the platform that supports our ambitions and pleasures.

At conversion our values change. The Bible contains many passages that speak to a change of values at conversion. One such passage is 2 Corinthians 5:17, used in chapter 3 to point out that all things become new at conversion. In the surrounding context Paul clarified the issues involved when we become new creations. Two are identified in verses 15-16:

> [Christ] died for all so that those who live should no longer live for themselves, but for the One who died for them and was raised. From now on, then, we do not know anyone in a purely human way. Even if we have known Christ in a purely human way, yet now we no longer know Him in this way.
>
> **2 CORINTHIANS 5:15-16**

THE WAY WE SEE OTHERS. In verse 15 Paul revealed that Christians have an obligation to live for the Christ who died for them. Christians value living for Christ because they've discovered real life in Him. In verse 16 Paul explained one of the major differences in perspective between non-Christians and Christians. Referring to his own experience, he disclosed that previously he'd measured people "in a purely human way." Literally, the Greek language says "according to the flesh," which means Paul had previously evaluated people in a normal, natural way. Valuing things in a natural way causes us to make artificial appraisals of people based on such factors as race, religion, and economic situation. This is the way we look at the world and appraise people when we see ourselves as the center of life.

When Paul became a Christian, he viewed people according to the Holy Spirit, who lived in him. Paul's understanding of the value of people now came from the Spirit.

THE WAY WE SEE JESUS. Before Paul was converted, he also viewed Christ through the lens of a natural perspective. No doubt this fueled his attempts to cleanse the world of Christians and of any trace of Jesus. As a rabbi and probably a member of the Sanhedrin, Paul agreed with those who found Jesus guilty of blasphemy. He perceived Jesus to be a troublemaker. Viewing Jesus "in a purely human way" meant he couldn't receive God's evaluation of Jesus, nor could he grasp that Jesus was God's Messiah.

A relationship with Christ changed that perspective. As a Christian, Paul valued Christ according to the Holy Spirit, not the flesh.

How does being a Christian change your values in life?

How does being a Christian change the way you view people?

Second Corinthians 5 goes on to say that a relationship with Christ makes all things new:

> If anyone is in Christ, he is a new creation;
> old things have passed away, and look, new things have come.
> **2 CORINTHIANS 5:17**

Conversion brings a comprehensive change in a Christian's outlook. Before we were saved, our worldview and value system revolved around three points.

1. We were naturally prone to put ourselves first.

2. We lived in a context of time, locked in history and movement. We couldn't embrace eternal qualities that didn't have roots in time.

3. We sought our own comfort. Therefore, things that made life safer, more secure, easier, or more fun had value. If anyone touched our things or possessions, they touched us deeply.

How do these three points describe your life before Christ?

You put yourself first:

You were locked in time:

You sought your own comfort:

These values may not be comprehensive, but they definitely represent the core of an unregenerate person. Holiness, in contrast, means living by God's value system rather than our own, accepting God's patterns for life rather than the world's. The following discussion illustrates ways our values change when we meet Christ.

GOD OVER SELF

The most radical and fundamental way people change when they accept Christ is to move from egocentricity to the centrality of God. Everything changes. Many passages affirm this core change.

The Gospels include a variety of references to the need to put God first in our lives. In Luke Jesus explained the cost of discipleship this way:

> Every one of you who does not say good-bye
> to all his possessions cannot be My disciple.

LUKE 14:33

That statement, when taken at face value, is radical, but it's consistent with the teaching Jesus had developed in that context. In verse 26 He identified potential barriers to following Christ: father and mother, brother and sister, wife and children, and one's own life. No doubt these seemed harsh words to those listening. In this instance Jesus' point was that a person who loves his family more than he loves God can't participate in God's kingdom. Family values can be properly appreciated when loving God and following Christ come first.

In writing to the church at Philippi, the apostle Paul explained his own pilgrimage to counter those who built their lives on the world's value system.

Read Philippians 3:4-14. What credentials enhanced Paul's status in the eyes of the world before he was saved?

How did his values change after he met Christ?

Paul's background was impeccable. He identified his heredity (see v. 5) and what he'd attained through his own achievements (see vv. 5-6). No one in Paul's world could fault those credentials. Yet both had led him down the wrong path, for his ambitions hadn't included Christ.

At conversion Paul's values changed radically. Verses 7-8 explain the change. Paul reached a point where he considered these things hindrances to gaining Christ. He used a Greek expression showing purpose to demonstrate that he gave up one so that he could gain the other. Neither heredity nor achievement is necessarily wrong. The problem was that Paul had trusted in them instead of Christ. Once he was converted, however, the greatest value in his life was knowing Christ (see v. 10).

When we're saved, God becomes more important than anything else in our lives—even more important than life itself. This change in values demonstrates itself in the desire to know Christ, be like Christ, and be with Christ. The practical outworking of this priority is revealed in a life that grows progressively more holy and more renewed in the image of its Creator. Millions of Christians have testified that they've experienced greater joy and fulfillment in placing Christ first in their lives and in submitting to the lordship of Jesus.

How has knowing Christ brought greater joy and fulfillment to your life?

If you've struggled to place Christ first in your life, what keeps you from making that commitment?

ETERNITY OVER TIME

The second way our values change when we're converted is that God calls us to place priority on things that are eternal over things that are temporal. This means seeking the kingdom of God instead of the things of this world.

Philosophers have long debated whether there's an afterlife and, if so, what it's like. The secular conclusions of the 20th century led us to one of two positions.

1. There's no afterlife.

2. We can't know about the afterlife, so we should live for the present.

Both of these conclusions have led people to focus on here and now as opposed to then and there. Merchandisers popularize these conclusions, convincing the world that this life and its values are all we really know. They encourage us to make the most of this life while we can since, from their perspective, the possibility of life after death is highly unlikely. Consequently, few people today have a perspective beyond time.

The root of this secular perspective is an anti-God bias. The basic questions are whether there's a God and, if so, whether we can know Him. Although most people believe God must exist, some philosophers have reached radically different conclusions. In their view, people who live for eternity rather than time are bizarre or odd.

Read the following Scriptures and record what each passage teaches about eternity.

Hebrews 2:14-15

Hebrews 9:27

The Bible continually warns us that an afterlife and a judgment will follow this life (see Heb. 9:27). Further, it teaches that we can't live this life properly unless we can solve the problem of death and the afterlife (see Heb. 2:15). Therefore, the change of focus from time to eternity is a necessary step in achieving holiness.

Many of Jesus' parables emphasized an eternal focus. For example, in Luke 12:13-21 Jesus told the parable of the rich fool. The man prospered in his business, so he decided to tear down his barns and build bigger ones. He desired the security that material possessions provide. But he took no thought for spiritual security. Then the man died and entered a world for which he was totally unprepared—the afterlife. In conclusion Jesus said:

> That's how it is with the one who stores up treasure
> for himself and is not rich toward God.
>
> **LUKE 12:21**

Jesus illustrated the truth even more graphically when He told the parable of the shrewd manager (see Luke 16:1-15). The manager was warned that he'd lose his job for improper management, so the man reduced the debt of the master's creditors. His rationale was that they'd appreciate him, and when he had no job, at least he'd have friends. In the story the master commended the manager for his shrewdness, but when we read the parable today, we struggle with what appears to be an unethical situation.

Yet Jesus acknowledged the dishonesty of the manager and didn't commend him for his dishonest actions. Jesus summarized the parable by challenging His disciples to "use worldly wealth" to gain entrance "into eternal dwellings" (v. 9, NIV). The story contrasts the values of time with those of eternity. Jesus wanted the disciples—and us—to realize that one day we too will lose the security earth affords. Since that time is inevitable, we'd be wise to use the assets of time to prepare for eternity.

What are some ways believers can use worldly assets to prepare for eternity?

The epistles also contain repeated examples of this point. The apostle Paul spoke about this issue. People who opposed his ministry questioned him about his life and his call to serve God. Paul answered them in 2 Corinthians 4:7-18, referring to the persecutions and hardships he'd endured to bring the gospel to them (see vv. 7-12). He spoke of his own decaying body, contrasted with the growth of his inner spirit (see vv. 16-17). Paul expressed his motivation in verses 17-18:

> Our momentary light affliction is producing for us an
> absolutely incomparable eternal weight of glory. So we do
> not focus on what is seen, but on what is unseen. For what
> is seen is temporary, but what is unseen is eternal.
>
> **2 CORINTHIANS 4:17-18**

This passage compares eternity to physical well-being. One of our greatest values is health. Even so, living for eternity is more important than maintaining health on earth.

The apostle James warned his readers about a preoccupation with the values of earth instead of the values of heaven. He envisioned a group of businessmen making plans for the expansion of their business (see Jas. 4:13-17). Their basic problem was the assumption that life would go on and that they could transact their business indefinitely. James warned about an arrogant life plan that disregards God and then offered a corrective:

> Instead, you should say, "If the Lord wills,
> we will live and do this or that."
>
> **JAMES 4:15**

Once again the Bible commends a worldview that considers eternity more important than time or success on earth.

What are some ways you can maintain an eternal perspective as you live your daily life?

We must acknowledge that when we focus on eternity, it's easy to move to the opposite extreme. Many Christians live so much for eternity that they neglect their responsibilities in time, assuming God will take care of responsibilities He's delegated to them. Not so. The Bible commends a balanced life. In fact, we're instructed to take care of family, health, and work responsibilities.

Yet the fact remains that none of these things are as important as preparing for eternity. God urges us to be realistic about life. Because He created us as eternal beings, life includes time, but more important, it includes eternity. A wise person orchestrates the affairs of life to center on God and His eternal kingdom priorities.

PEOPLE OVER THINGS

The third area revealing the change in value systems at conversion is the value of people over things. This is radically different from the world's perspective. Our world values people as long as they don't interfere with personal goals and security—the exact opposite of God's value system.

Again, the Gospels and the epistles illustrate this change. One day Jesus encountered a young man of wealth and position (see Luke 18:18-30). To the man's credit he also had spiritual interests. He wanted to enter the kingdom of God, so he inquired of Jesus about it. What could he do? Jesus' words pierced to the heart of the problem: "Sell all that you have and distribute it to the poor" (v. 22). Jesus put his finger on the man's basic problem: the man loved his wealth more than he loved God. A second issue also presented itself: the man loved his money more than he loved people. In his refusal to do what Jesus instructed, the man revealed that he had the same problem with both God and people. His values were wrong.

What are some ways the world values things over people?

How did Jesus' life demonstrate that He cared more about people than things?

Jesus didn't require everyone who inquired about entering the kingdom to sell everything they owned. Nevertheless, every person possesses something difficult to release, even for God's kingdom. The numerous passages in which Jesus urged His followers to consider the poor reveal a basic kingdom value: God cares more for people than He cares for things. Jesus demonstrated this priority by leaving heaven to come to earth and die for people. Christians should embrace the same values.

The apostle Paul also emphasized people over things. An example is 1 Corinthians 9, where he defended his rights as an apostle to the church at Corinth.

Read 1 Corinthians 9:3-14. What rights did Paul mention that he wasn't taking advantage of?

How does this passage illustrate that Paul valued people more than things?

Rather than focus on his rights, Paul focused on his responsibilities. Even though he had a right to a wife and support from the church, he did without both (see vv. 3-14). He knew financial gain could interfere with his ministry. He also knew marriage would be unwise for him because of his ministry responsibilities. Paul clearly understood that people are more important than money and personal privileges.

These examples illustrate the changed value system that occurs at conversion. Most Christians don't realize that following Christ will radically change their lives. Generally, we come to Christ from our deep need, hoping He will meet us and deliver us from our immediate concerns. Regardless of what prompts our movement to accept Christ, no one comes to Him without a sense of personal weakness and failure. With our recognition of failure comes a willingness to change our ways to His. We believe God will give us a better life than we have, and He does just that.

Not all Christians live according to God's values. However, from the moment we come to Christ, the Spirit of God urges believers to accept these new attitudes. Frustration builds, in part, because the Holy Spirit directs His energy toward producing these changes in us, and we don't always willingly embrace them. That frustration is relieved only when we live in harmony with the Holy Spirit and yield to His leadership.

The bottom line is that salvation brings a new value system. God expects us to accept His values. When we do, we have spiritual success, and we grow in the likeness of Jesus. At the heart of His value system are the truths that God is more important than self, eternity is more important than time, and people are more important than things.

Mark the scales to indicate your growth toward new Christian values.

1	2	3	4	5	6	7	8	9	10

I value self over God.   *I value God over self.*

1	2	3	4	5	6	7	8	9	10

I'm focused on time.   *I'm focused on eternity.*

1	2	3	4	5	6	7	8	9	10

I value things over people.   *I value people over things.*

What actions will you take to grow in kingdom values?

AMBITIONS OF THE CHRISTIAN LIFE

At conversion God changes our hearts so that we possess new ambitions. Ambitions are internal actions to achieve what we value. Evaluating our personal ambitions can reveal whether we're living like a Christian or like a non-Christian. The values of God, eternity, and people motivate us to a different lifestyle from the values of self and things.

Scripture reveals at least five ambitions that characterize mature Christians. Not all Christians live by these, but God intends us to do so, and the Holy Spirit seeks to encourage them in us. As we respond to the Spirit's leading, we devote our energies to the following ambitions: worship, Christian lifestyle, stewardship, ministry, and family relationships.

WORSHIP

Worship is at the heart of all Christian activity. *Worship* means *to appreciate God for who He is and to enjoy Him for what He does.* Jesus taught us how to worship. In His encounter with the Samaritan woman at the well, He spoke of worship (see John 4:1-42). One issue that separated the Jews from the Samaritans was the place of worship. Jews worshiped at the Jerusalem temple, while Samaritans worshiped at the Samaritan temple. Jesus explained that with His coming, He brought a new dimension to worship. Up until that time, the place of worship was important. With His coming, the spirit of worship, rather than the place of worship, became primary. He taught:

> True worshipers will worship the Father in spirit and truth.
> Yes, the Father wants such people to worship Him.
>
> **JOHN 4:23**

Worship in spirit and truth demands the involvement of the entire person. It calls for consistency of word and action and the total commitment of every facet of the person to God. Because the Father seeks worshipers, putting God before self means, in part, that we fill our minds with the worship of God, communicating with Him in spirit and truth. Pure, effective worship is one of the highest ambitions of a believer.

What's your response to the statement that "worship is at the heart of all Christian activity"?

What does it mean for a believer to worship in spirit and truth?

CHRISTIAN LIFESTYLE

The ambition to live a consistent Christian lifestyle grows from new values. Translating our beliefs into practical, everyday living is always a challenge. In fact, much of the New Testament, especially Paul's epistles, addresses that very issue. The epistles are corrective in nature (see 1 Cor. 5:9-11, referring to a letter written prior to 1 Cor.; also see Gal. 1:6-9). Other letters, however, respond to questions about how to live the Christian life. For example, Paul wrote 1 Corinthians in response to a visit from Christians in Corinth who reported their situation and asked questions the congregation had raised about theological issues (see 1 Cor. 7:1).

Read 1 Corinthians 5:9-11 and Galatians 1:6-9. What areas of Christian living did Paul address?

Jesus anticipated the issue of Christian living when He delivered His famous Sermon on the Mount (see Matt. 5–7). Much of the sermon discusses Christians' proper attitudes and relationships. For practical, everyday living the central passage is Matthew 6:25-34. In this passage Jesus addressed the issues of food and health (see v. 25), clothes (see v. 28), and life itself (see vv. 27,34). These everyday matters can cause people to worry, and our response to them reveals a major difference between God's people and non-Christians (see vv. 32-33).

Jesus provided two principles for Christian living in Matthew 6:33

> Seek first the kingdom of God and His righteousness,
> and all these things will be provided for you.
>
> **MATTHEW 6:33**

1. God's people should seek His kingdom as a priority. This directive restates the new value of God over self. Rather than entertain concerns that occupy our thoughts and energy as non-Christians, we're to devote our lives and energies to God's concerns. A Christian's primary concerns are God's kingdom and personal righteousness.

2. God's people should trust God for His provision. Jesus contrasted the frantic activity of pagans (they "eagerly seek all these things," v. 32) with the quiet assurance of Christians ("your heavenly Father knows," v. 32). His words speak to the lifestyle of His people. We trust God for life and the provisions of life, and we place a greater priority on the kingdom of God than on personal concerns.

What are some persistent worries in your life?

How does Matthew 6:33 put those worries into perspective?

These themes of Christian living repeatedly occur in the epistles as well. In responding to specific life issues, the writers addressed personal commitment to God's will, as well as trusting God for life's needs. Regarding the first, Paul often urged Christians to develop Christian purity and character.

Read the following verses and summarize Paul's commands for living.

1 Thessalonians 4:3

Ephesians 4:1

Philippians 2:5

Philippians 3:12-14

Other New Testament writers presented the same theme. The writer of Hebrews urged his readers to develop Christian maturity (see 6:1); to approach God with genuineness, purity, faith, and hope (see 10:19-25); and to be holy (see 12:14). James reminded his readers to display wisdom in good deeds (see 3:13) and of the necessity of clean hands and pure hearts (see 4:8). Peter called his readers to seek holiness as God "is holy" (1 Pet. 1:15), to pursue clean and pure lives (see 2:11-12), and to escape "the corruption that is in the world" (2 Pet. 1:4). The apostle John, writing near the end of his life, encouraged second- and third-generation Christians to overcome sin (see 1 John 2:1), to keep God's commandments (see 2:3), to overcome the world (see 2:15-17; 4:4), and to imitate "what is good" (3 John 11). Growing in the character of Jesus and expressing our Christian faith in our everyday lives are prominent teachings throughout the New Testament.

STEWARDSHIP

The third illustration of the new ambitions characterizing a Christian is stewardship. Biblical stewardship is an issue that affects all of life, not just money. God wants us to use all we have and all we are for His purposes. As we seek to live consistently, we develop a strong sense of stewardship for everything God has provided. God gives us all things, and the circumstances of life provide opportunities to be and do as God intends. As a good steward, each of us represents God in our own unique way.

Paul's account of the Macedonian churches' generosity in 2 Corinthians 8 demonstrates several qualities of stewardship:

> We want you to know, brothers, about the grace of God granted to the churches of Macedonia: During a severe testing by affliction, their abundance of joy and their deep poverty overflowed into the wealth of their generosity. I testify that, on their own, according to their ability and beyond their ability, they begged us insistently for the privilege of sharing in the ministry to the saints, and not just as we had hoped. Instead, they gave themselves especially to the Lord, then to us by God's will.
>
> **2 CORINTHIANS 8:1-5**

What motivated the Macedonians' generosity in giving?

What principles of stewardship do you see in the previous passage?

We can identify several principles of stewardship, based on this passage.

STEWARDSHIP IS A PRODUCT OF GOD'S GRACE. This grace was evident in two ways: God brought the Macedonian believers the grace of conversion, and as they lived out their response to grace, God continued to impress on them the opportunity to give. Giving was a matter of God's grace (see v. 1).

STEWARDSHIP BRINGS JOY. These believers joyfully responded to God's will and shared with others in need. Poverty didn't keep them from accomplishing what God desired for their lives (see v. 2). Though they experienced serious poverty, they found joy in giving.

STEWARDSHIP IS FELLOWSHIP WITH OTHER CHRISTIANS. The Macedonian believers well understood the interconnectedness of Christians as brothers and sisters. Their stewardship extended to others because of the privilege of sharing in their hardships (see v. 4).

STEWARDSHIP IS AN OUTWORKING OF DEVOTION. These churches were first committed to the Lord and second to the apostle Paul (see v. 5). Stewardship of life is a natural outworking of a deep commitment to God, one of a Christian's new ambitions.

Evaluate your stewardship, using the four previous principles. How does your stewardship compare to this biblical model?

MINISTRY

Ministry is the fourth ambition that expresses the new values of the Christian life. When we've met Christ, ministry becomes a priority and can take many forms. Not every Christian ministers in the same way, because we all have different spiritual gifts (see 1 Cor. 12). Even so, every obedient Christian desires to minister to other people. This inclination clearly emphasizes the value of people over things.

Jesus set a high example of self-giving service. He stated that He came for the purpose of serving others and that His followers must be servants as well:

Whoever wants to become great among you must be your servant, and whoever wants to be first among you must be a slave to all. For even the Son of Man did not come to be served, but to serve, and to give His life—a ransom for many.

MARK 10:43-45

Jesus' greatest illustration occurred the night before His crucifixion. In the upper room He commanded His disciples to be like Him—a servant (see John 13:13-16).

The epistles reinforce the necessity for Christians to minister to others. On several occasions Paul described his life purpose in terms of service:

Even if I am poured out as a drink offering on the sacrifice and service of your faith, I am glad and rejoice with all of you.

PHILIPPIANS 2:17

Ministry was also an important theme in Paul's teachings.

What do the following verses teach about Christian service?

Romans 12:9-10; 13:8-10

Romans 12:17-21

1 Corinthians 12:27-31

Paul advocated the priority of love for others (see Rom. 12:9-10; 13:8-10), not returning evil when evil is done to you (see Rom. 12:17-21), and serving the Lord and the church by exercising the gifts of the Spirit (see 1 Cor. 12:27-31).

The Holy Spirit urges Christians to minister. He equips and directs us so that we can maximize our contribution to the kingdom as well as represent Christ to the unsaved world. Ministry is one of our new ambitions following conversion, reflecting our new value of giving priority to people over things.

FAMILY RELATIONSHIPS

The final expression of a Christian's new ambitions is a renewed interest in the family. When we start following Christ, we soon learn that God has a plan for the family. God ordained the family—husband, wife, and children. He established clear guidelines for family organization and relationships. Spiritual interest in the family begins at conversion, and often one family member is instrumental in leading others to Christ.

One natural outworking of salvation is a desire for the family to be what God intended when He originally established it in the garden of Eden. The family is God's way to nurture, respect, and rear children. It provides for emotionally well-rounded persons, for the deepest levels of social interaction, and for a conducive environment to nurture the maturing process.

However, there's a deeper dimension to Christian family life. God wants the family to be like Him. It should be the closest place to heaven on earth. In a family that functions according to God's will and follows His Word, members learn how to relate to one another from the security and self-understanding that come from knowing their identity in Christ. This requires that each member intentionally strive to grow in Christlikeness.

Family members also learn spiritual truths that can be learned only from building the close relationships demanded in family life. Because the family is the place where the most intimate relationships occur, it can be a place where the character and ways of God are revealed. Individual family members see one another's imperfections, as well as their own, and they rejoice in the growth of others. Further, the family represents God to the world. When others observe the Christian family, they should be impressed with its love for one another, as well as the supporting spiritual foundation.

Who has encouraged you in your Christian walk and nurtured you in your spiritual growth? How did they encourage you?

The Holy Spirit encourages us to develop the ambition of having properly functioning, spiritually powerful families. This occurs as the family spends time together developing common interests and goals, as well as praying, studying the Bible, and ministering together. These experiences offer the joy of fellowship at the deepest of human relationships and are heightened by the presence of the Lord Himself. The Christian family is a powerful witness to the world and one of the highest and most rewarding of all goals and ambitions.

Describe how you've grown in developing the following ambitions since becoming a Christian.

Worship:

Christian lifestyle:

Stewardship:

Ministry:

Family relationships:

Identify an action you need to take after studying these ambitions of the Christian life.

PLEASURES OF THE CHRISTIAN LIFE

So far we've discussed two of the three changes that occur when we're saved.

1. God changes us so that we have new values.

2. Our new values lead to new ambitions.

Now let's explore the third change—new pleasures. Pleasures are the things we enjoy. Generally, our pleasures grow from our ambitions. The more we're able to achieve our ambitions, the more pleasure we derive from a particular activity or event. For example, if being in good physical shape is a value and a regular exercise program is an ambition, pleasure comes when we live according to that value and ambition. Acting on our value and ambition brings us satisfaction and joy, not to mention many other benefits.

If one of our values is to have a family that functions according to God's design, an ambition is to actively seek and promote God's will in our families. As we achieve this ambition, we experience pleasure. Parents and grandparents find satisfaction and joy when they observe their children and grandchildren choosing spiritual values or making God-honoring choices.

Pleasures bring satisfaction to the degree that they build on proper values and ambitions. If the basic value is wrong because it's short-lived or unwise, the effort to achieve it will be misspent. Any pleasure experienced will also be short-lived since, like the value on which it's based, it's temporary. That's why Scripture constantly instructs us to build our lives on the solid foundation of Christ. Jesus contrasted the foolish and wise men who build their houses on sand and rock, respectively:

> Everyone who hears these words of Mine and acts on them will
> be like a sensible man who built his house on the rock. The rain
> fell, the rivers rose, and the winds blew and pounded that house.
> Yet it didn't collapse, because its foundation was on the rock.
> But everyone who hears these words of Mine and doesn't act
> on them will be like a foolish man who built his house on the
> sand. The rain fell, the rivers rose, the winds blew and pounded
> that house, and it collapsed. And its collapse was great!
>
> **MATTHEW 7:24-27**

Paul exhorted Christians to live so that they'd receive appropriate rewards in heaven:

> If anyone builds on that foundation with gold, silver, costly stones,
> wood, hay, or straw, each one's work will become obvious, for the
> day will disclose it, because it will be revealed by fire; the fire will
> test the quality of each one's work. If anyone's work that he has built
> survives, he will receive a reward. If anyone's work is burned up, it will
> be lost, but he will be saved; yet it will be like an escape through fire.
>
> **1 CORINTHIANS 3:12-15**

Though these words primarily refer to the work of Christian ministers who build on Christ as the only proper foundation, the implication is that all Christians will give an account for their life's effort.

What values and ambitions are reflected in the two previous passages?

Read the following verses and identify the pleasures that bring lasting satisfaction.

Psalm 1:2

Colossians 3:1-2

Philippians 3:8-11

The Scriptures provide a strong indication about which pleasures bring lasting satisfaction. Psalm 1 praises the person whose "delight is in the Lord's instruction" (v. 2). God's Word brings pleasure because it can guide us into the lasting joys of life. In Colossians 3:1-2 Paul stated that the lordship of Jesus brings the maximum good. He used two synonyms to express the idea of acknolwedging Jesus lordship in our lives. Translated as "set your hearts on things above" and "set your minds on things above," these terms remind us that our successes and joys come from having a deep desire for and involvement with activities and possessions that honor Jesus. In expressing his own new ambitions, Paul spoke of an ongoing goal in life that brought him lasting satisfaction. He said in Philippians 3:8-11 that his new, all-consuming goal was "to know [Christ]." Every facet of Paul's experience grew from his desire to know Jesus well and to attain the joy of the resurrection from the dead.

As Christians walk with God and become more like Him, their pleasures change. They derive increasing satisfaction from achieving success in living by their new values.

Identify the values and ambitions that bring you pleasure in life. Categorize them as worldly or godly goals.

Worldly   *Godly*

Write a value and an ambition you'll pursue that will bring you greater joy in knowing Christ.

Value:

Ambition:

When people are converted, they gain a new spiritual interest and direction. That's the distinctive difference between the old life and the new life. Although not all Christians immediately realize all the changes in their lives, regeneration brings a new openness to God, and the Holy Spirit brings new insights and motivations. Life is lived with sensitivity to God, eternity, and other people. These changes lead to spiritual ambitions in worship, ministry, Christian living, stewardship, and family relationships.

Sometimes people live compartmentalized lives, separating their Christian faith from other aspects of life. They wonder what interest God has in work, recreation, financial security, or other "secular" activities. But such compartmentalization fails to grasp the fact that God saves the entire person. Every aspect of life becomes different when Jesus is Lord. Why? Because He is Lord of all. Even routine demands of the past and of everyday living are energized with new responsibility and power.

We need to recognize the changes brought by new life in Christ so that we can effectively pursue holiness. As we mature in Christ, we'll become more like Him. The values, ambitions, and pleasures of the old person will be replaced by the values, ambitions, and pleasures of the new person. This doesn't occur overnight, but we should have an awareness of what the Holy Spirit intends in our lives so that we're ready to respond to His leading and cooperate with the changes He works to bring.

This chapter focused on principles that shape the new life in Christ, not specific activities. It's impossible to provide a list of what to do when. Even if such a list could be provided, that isn't God's intent. God intends for His people to understand the biblical principles of their new lives and use those principles to respond to the issues that present themselves at any time or in any situation. In the process of sanctification, God relates to us personally, leading us along in ways that are appropriate to His will and purposes. It's our privilege to live out the principles to pursue holy lives.

So far we've discussed what holiness is and what happens at conversion to set us on a path to holiness. We've also considered principles for Christian living and incentive for spiritual growth. But knowing these things won't make us holy; more is required. The remaining chapters will discuss how to live successfully as holy followers of Christ.

How do you see the Holy Spirit leading you to live a holy life and to grow in the likeness of Jesus?

What do you need to change in order to cooperate with the Spirit's work in your life?

Pray and ask God to work in you to bring your values, ambitions, and pleasures into alignment with His will and His Word.

CHAPTER 4 GROUP EXPERIENCE
WHAT'S NEW ABOUT A CHRISTIAN?

COMING TOGETHER

1. *What conflicts of values did you experience after becoming a Christian? Think about areas like work, priorities, recreation, choice of friends, and use of time.*

2. *How did God lead you to make new choices after you were saved?*

VALUES OF THE CHRISTIAN LIFE

1. *Read the following verses.*

[Christ] died for all so that those who live should no longer live for themselves, but for the One who died for them and was raised. From now on, then, we do not know anyone in a purely human way. Even if we have known Christ in a purely human way, yet now we no longer know Him in this way. Therefore, if anyone is in Christ, he is a new creation; old things have passed away, and look, new things have come.

2 CORINTHIANS 5:15-17

How does being a Christian change the way you see Jesus? The way you see others?

2. *What are some ways you would characterize an unbeliever's values?*

3. *How does being saved cause you to value God over yourself?*

4. Read the following verses.

Our momentary light affliction is producing for us an
absolutely incomparable eternal weight of glory. So we do
not focus on what is seen, but on what is unseen. For what
is seen is temporary, but what is unseen is eternal.

2 CORINTHIANS 4:17-18

*How does being saved shift your focus from time to eternity? Give examples
of how that might change a believer's values.*

*5. Recall the account of the rich man in Luke 18:18-30. What does this
encounter indicate about the man's values?*

6. How does following Jesus change the way you value other people?

AMBITIONS OF THE CHRISTIAN LIFE

1. How did your ambitions change when you became a believer?

*2. Discuss the following questions about the new ambitions
of the Christian life.*

• Read John 4:23.

An hour is coming, and is now here, when the true
worshipers will worship the Father in spirit and truth.
Yes, the Father wants such people to worship Him.

Why does worship become a primary ambition after someone is saved?

• Read Matthew 6:33.

Seek first the kingdom of God and His righteousness,
and all these things will be provided for you.

What principles did Jesus provide for the ambition of Christian living?
What are some of your favorite Scripture passages that guide you
in Christian living?

• Read 2 Corinthians 8:1-5. What principles can you identify for the
ambition of stewardship?

• Read Mark 10:43-45. Why is ministry a godly ambition for a believer?
What are some ways Christians can minister?

• Read Ephesians 5:28-32. How can family relationships mirror God's design?
How did your family relationships change after you were saved?

PLEASURES OF THE CHRISTIAN LIFE

1. How does pleasure relate to our values and ambitions?

2. How have your pleasures changed since you became a believer?

3. Read the following verses.

His delight is in the LORD's instruction,
and he meditates on it day and night.

PSALM 1:2

If you have been raised with the Messiah, seek what is above, where the Messiah is, seated at the right hand of God. Set your minds on what is above, not on what is on the earth.

COLOSSIANS 3:1-2

I also consider everything to be a loss in view of the surpassing value of knowing Christ Jesus my Lord. Because of Him I have suffered the loss of all things and consider them filth, so that I may gain Christ and be found in Him, not having a righteousness of my own from the law, but one that is through faith in Christ— the righteousness from God based on faith. My goal is to know Him and the power of His resurrection and the fellowship of His sufferings, being conformed to His death, assuming that I will somehow reach the resurrection from among the dead.

PHILIPPIANS 3:8-11

According to these verses, what pursuits bring lasting pleasure in the Christian life?

4. *How have you experienced God working to change your values, ambitions, and pleasures over the years?*

5. *Ask God to help you pursue values, ambitions, and pleasures that align with His Word and that give evidence of new life in Christ.*

CHAPTER 5
EFFECTING CHANGE

In 1864 President Abraham Lincoln issued the Emancipation Proclamation, which proclaimed freedom for slaves in America. The Emancipation Proclamation served to rally the North and hasten the end of the war, as well as the terrible practice of human slavery in the United States.

The proclamation was great news, but many questions remained. The war was still being fought, and Confederate troops still occupied many areas of the South. The basic question for a slave who heard the proclamation was "Am I really free?"

When we receive new life in Christ, God says we're holy, free from sin, and capable of having complete fellowship with Him. Yet there's a major difference between being declared holy—free from sin's power in life—and actually being holy. Having decided to side with God over evil, a new Christian has entered the battle of the ages. There are spiritual attacks from the outside, and there are habits, fears, lusts, and pressures on the inside. The question for Christians is, Am I really holy?

How do you answer the previous question?

Give the basis for your answer.

The slaves of 1864 were legally free. But what would it take for them to actually be free? There were three essential steps to realizing that freedom, and they give us a clear picture of the steps for realizing holiness in a believer's life.

1. The slaves would have to possess the knowledge that the Emancipation Proclamation provided for their freedom. Without knowledge of the proclamation, the slaves could live in slavery indefinitely.

2. The slaves would have to make difficult choices they'd never been allowed to make. They didn't know how to live as free people, nor did they have the necessary resources to begin living a life of freedom. First they must choose to gather their belongings and families, then exercise the newly promised freedom to walk away from the plantation, and finally choose a new life.

3. The slaves would require power. They'd faced the power exerted by the masters to keep them as slaves. Other slave owners and the entire army of the South could force them back to their masters. To achieve real freedom, the slaves needed resources beyond themselves.

A Christian must take similar steps to live a holy life in Christ. This chapter explores the three basic issues confronting Christians in their daily battle for holiness: knowledge, choices, and power.

KNOWLEDGE

The basic foundation for change is knowledge. God works primarily in and through the mind. Almost all Christian growth begins with some understanding of certain issues, life patterns, and possibilities. Once the mind is confident in its convictions, it's able to influence the rest of the person to choose what's right.

THE MIND IN THE NEW TESTAMENT

Scripture frequently addresses the significance of the mind in personal transformation. The Greek word for *mind, noos,* occurs 24 times in the New Testament, 12 of which are in Paul's epistles. Paul's discussion fits the general tenor of Scripture that people live as their minds instruct. Sometimes the word conveys the meaning of *understanding—the faculty of being able to think.* In this sense Paul stated that he'd rather not speak in tongues because while doing so, his "understanding is unfruitful" (1 Cor. 14:14). It's better to use the mind to worship God.

Read the following verses and record what Paul taught about the mind.

Romans 1:28

Philippians 4:7

2 Thessalonians 2:1-2

Paul warned of being shaken in the mind by misunderstanding theology (see 2 Thess. 2:1-2). Further, he indicated that God's peace surpasses the tendency to dwell on specific fears (see Phil. 4:7). Paul warned of Gentiles whom God had allowed to pursue depraved or reprobate thoughts (see Rom. 1:28).

One characteristic of persons without Christ is that they use their minds for things other than the interests of God (see Eph. 4:17; Col. 2:18). Consequently, they have depraved and unclean minds (see 2 Tim. 3:8; Titus 1:15). One of God's major works in conversion is to change the mind so that people can embrace God's truth.

Identify a major way God has changed your thinking since you became a Christian.

The concept of depravity can be confusing. In everyday conversations we speak of depraved people as those who commit the most hideous, extreme sins. But in the Bible the word isn't used with such a restricted meaning. The Bible uses the term *depraved* to mean *cut off from God*. The depraved mind doesn't have the light of God's Holy Spirit within and therefore centers all the issues of life around itself. The term describes the blindness sin produces in all of us that leads to sinful actions.

Yet in spite of their depravity, even unsaved people can do good things because of the inner impulse that comes from being created in the image of God. Paul explained:

> When Gentiles, who do not have the law, instinctively do what the law demands, they are a law to themselves even though they do not have the law. They show that the work of the law is written on their hearts. Their consciences confirm this.
>
> **ROMANS 2:14-15**

Moral people are quite capable of deriving appropriate standards of living. When they reason together with others who seek to live consistently moral lives, they clarify and accept even higher standards (see Rom. 2:1-16). In Romans 2:17-29 Paul discussed the situation of religious people, using the Jewish heritage as the prime example. Today some unsaved people own a Bible, read it, and value it. The issue for them is whether they live up to it.

Paul acknowledged that at times people can and do choose to live correctly. Because they make correct choices on occasion, they possess enough knowledge to value proper choices and good moral conduct. Yet being able to recognize and value moral and religious conduct makes us responsible to live consistently moral and religious lives. When we fail to live up to these standards, we reveal that we're candidates for God's judgment.

Paul summarized his discussion on everyone's need for salvation in Romans 3:9-20.

*Read Romans 3:9-20. What are some attitudes and actions Paul named
to illustrate human depravity?*

Do you think Paul's description is applicable today? Why or why not?

Using multiple Old Testament texts to prove his point, Paul explained that no one does good, no one seeks God, and all people are self-centered. This is the biblical meaning of *depravity*. Depravity is living without regard to God's will for our lives. All people naturally live that way. Therefore, we know the unredeemed mind is corrupt and depraved.

Perhaps the central passage devoted to the importance of the mind is Romans 12:1-2. After presenting Scripture's most theologically precise discussion of salvation, the apostle Paul turned his thoughts to practical matters of Christian living. He stated:

> Brothers, by the mercies of God, I urge you to present your
> bodies as a living sacrifice, holy and pleasing to God; this is
> your spiritual worship. Do not be conformed to this age, but
> be transformed by the renewing of your mind, so that you may
> discern what is the good, pleasing, and perfect will of God.
>
> **ROMANS 12:1-2**

The terms *present, sacrifice, holy and pleasing to God,* and *spiritual worship* come from the sacrificial language and imagery of Israel. This passage speaks directly to the point of personal holiness—being separated to God.

*Why would offering your body as a sacrifice to God be a vital step in renewing
your mind?*

The relationship between mind and body is of primary importance for our study. Paul contrasted the two, suggesting that he conceived of the body as the mind's implementer. The body does what the mind thinks. Paul anticipated this teaching in Romans 6:11-14, in which he urged his readers to present their bodies to God—body parts and human characteristics—to avoid using the body for evil. It's clear that our minds are the instruments that control our bodies.

Romans 12:1-2 explains that offering the body to the Lord includes the mind but also reveals the tension described so many times in this book. We're to present our bodies as "holy and pleasing to God" (Rom. 12:1). This verse refers to the initial act of separating ourselves to God for His purposes. But actual holiness requires more than making a climactic commitment to God. What was previously unholy must become holy. There must be personal transformation, and that occurs in the renewing of the mind (see v. 2).

Paul used two picturesque images in these verses.

1. The first picture is of a mold or form: "Do not be conformed to this age" (v. 2). An unbeliever lives in a constant pattern of conformity. The world shapes everyone into a mold. This shaping comes from external pressures of the environment, but it also comes from personal participation in the world's values and activities:

   Each person is tempted when he is drawn away and enticed by his own evil desires. Then after desire has conceived, it gives birth to sin, and when sin is fully grown, it gives birth to death.
   JAMES 1:14-15

We naturally and willingly participate in the world's values because of the world's affinity with our minds.

2. The second picture is of a metamorphosis: "Be transformed by the renewing of your mind" (Rom. 12:2). The literal picture is of a butterfly undergoing a metamorphosis, a change of form that begins inside and works its way out. A believer can be transformed. In contrast to the external pressures that squeeze us into conformity with the world, if the mind is changed, it has the capacity to change the entire person. Thus, a change from within (in the mind) works its way out (in the body).

The actual transformation of a person is proportionate to the renewing of the mind. The mind doesn't immediately change on conversion. Mental habits take time to change. The mind must understand and embrace the needed changes, as well as grasp a plan for making them. But the apostle John encouraged his readers to keep pursuing holy lives by reminding them, "You have an anointing from the Holy One, and all of you have knowledge" (1 John 2:20). At conversion God begins the process of renewal by building on our knowledge of Christ. This renewal process was previously discussed in connection with the old person/new person theology.

Reread Romans 12:1-2. In what ways do you offer your body "as a living sacrifice … to God" (v. 1)?

In what ways do you seek to "be transformed by the renewing of your mind" (v. 2)?

CONTRASTING WAYS OF LIFE

One way to help the mind grasp the things of God is to contrast God's will and the world's way. We do this by studying God's Word. Many biblical texts illustrate this contrast by addressing specific life issues that make the differences concrete. These passages demonstrate two things.

1. The differences between God's way of living and the world's way

2. How Christians can evaluate their walk with God

Jesus frequently illustrated these contrasts. In the Sermon on the Mount, He contrasted what others said with what He said (see Matt. 5:21,27,31,33,38,43). He indicated the differences between people who try to gain position or popularity by their religious activity and those whose actions are lived for Christ (see Matt. 6:1-18). Further, He warned of the folly of those who build their lives on human wisdom rather than on God's (see Matt. 7:24-27).

The epistles also contrast the two ways of living. Almost the entire New Testament contrasts sinfulness and holiness, but specific passages spotlight the differences between Christians and non-Christians. Passages like 1 Corinthians 6:9-11, Galatians 5:19-24, Ephesians 4:25–5:17, Colossians 3:5-17, 2 Timothy 3, and James 3:13-18 demonstrate the two ways of living. The contrasts often present extremes, characterizing unbelievers at their worst and believers at their best. Observing the extremes of non-Christian behavior warns us to do whatever we can to avoid them. Observing the benefits of a Christian lifestyle encourages us to follow God's will and to seek to become like Christ.

Read the following Scriptures and identify areas of life that require a change of mind if we're to pursue holiness.

Matthew 5:21,27,31,33,38,43

1 Corinthians 6:9-11

Galatians 5:19-24

Which of these areas remind you of ways God has transformed your mind?

PRINCIPLES OF CHRISTIAN GROWTH

Gaining knowledge or renewing the mind also requires knowing and implementing biblical principles of Christian growth. The starting point for all Christian growth is the conversion experience. The Holy Spirit convicts the unregenerate mind of sin. As people recognize and become convicted about their sin, they cry out to God for help: "I'll do anything to escape the sin that's destroying my life." God says, "You can't do anything, but I can. In fact, I already have. I've sent Jesus."

God's mercy provides a way of escape. As the unbelieving sinner embraces Jesus, the Savior, the mind affirms two changes that need to take place.

1. The desire to change patterns of thinking about God, sin, and self. This is repentance.

2. The desire to allow Jesus to reconstruct the person's life

Although not all people recognize the full implications of accepting Jesus as Savior, in time these attitudes are clarified. The point is that repentance, faith, and embracing Jesus all make a person predisposed to a holy life as a believer.

How did your conversion create a desire in you to live a holy life?

Romans 6:1-14 clearly explains the experience of new life in Christ. Paul discussed the possibility that Christians might entertain the idea of continuing to sin since their salvation is ensured. Such a desire is unthinkable. Paul said, "Absolutely not!" (v. 2). It's also unnatural to a life that's dead to sin (see vv. 2-10). In refuting the idea, Paul took Christians back to their conversion. We've been crucified with Christ, identifying with Him in death and resurrection. We've been spiritually baptized into Christ, which means God considers us one with Jesus. We share in all His experiences (see vv. 4-11).

The shared experience with Christ includes both death and resurrection. In sharing His death, we died to sin as He did. We no longer live with sin as the ruling power in our lives. Recognizing that fact leads to an understanding of freedom from sin. As crucified people, we don't have to submit to sin's influence, power, or destiny.

Sharing in Christ's experience also means participating in His resurrection. Just as He rose, we rose from our death to sin. We now have the power to live a new life with God as King. Sin no longer dominates our lives. God replaces Satan. Righteousness replaces sin. Eternal life replaces death. Our crucifixion with Christ at the conversion experience provides the basis of a new life—positionally and practically. Realizing the implications of that—the fact of our justification from sin—enables us to choose new directions for life.

How does the picture of dying to sin and rising to new life in Christ affect your thinking about living the Christian life?

CHOICES

To grow in holiness, people need more than knowledge. Holy living also depends on proper choices. Accurate knowledge comes from understanding what the Bible teaches. Proper choices require a different type of skill. The world is full of people whose broken lives and failed relationships reveal the difficulty of making correct choices. The fact is that we'll become what we choose to become. Choices make life what it is.

CHOICES PROMOTING HOLINESS

The Bible powerfully speaks on the subject of choices. Myriads of Old and New Testament commands relate to every conceivable aspect of life, always focusing on principles that will bring the joy that comes from holy living.

CHOOSING SALVATION. Many factors lead a person to salvation. Jesus did His part in dying for sinners, and the Holy Spirit convicts and leads people to confess Christ. On the other hand, the Bible clearly teaches there's no salvation without personal choice. Every individual must decide whether to choose Christ. Predicting the coming day of the Lord, the prophet Joel prophesied a universal availability of salvation to those who would call on the Lord (see 2:32). Both Peter and Paul quoted that Old Testament verse when they urged people to accept Christ:

> Everyone who calls on the name of the Lord will be saved. And with many other words he testified and strongly urged them, saying, "Be saved from this corrupt generation!"
>
> **ACTS 2:21,40**

> Everyone who calls on the name of the Lord will be saved. But how can they call on Him they have not believed in? And how can they believe without hearing about Him? And how can they hear without a preacher?
>
> **ROMANS 10:13-14**

Peter and Paul affirmed that Jesus' death opened the day of salvation, but they realized that people had to choose God's gift of grace. The most important choice of all is the choice to accept Christ. Until that decision is made, nothing else really matters. Once it's made, a new life begins.

CHOOSING TOTAL COMMITMENT. A second choice that promotes holiness is choosing complete dedication to Christ. Normally, people make this dedication at the time of conversion. But some Christians reveal that for various reasons they didn't clearly understand this choice. Therefore, many completely dedicate themselves to God's will at another point after conversion.

Was the choice of total commitment a part of your conversion, or did you make this commitment at a later time? Why?

If you haven't yet made that total commitment to God, take time to pray about it. If you're ready, make that commitment now.

The Old Testament anticipates a total involvement of a person's life with God. One example is Joshua, the great leader of Israel. He called the people to consider whom they would serve:

> If it doesn't please you to worship Yahweh, choose for yourselves today the one you will worship: the gods your fathers worshiped beyond the Euphrates River or the gods of the Amorites in whose land you are living. As for me and my family, we will worship Yahweh.
>
> **JOSHUA 24:15**

In good leadership fashion Joshua unequivocally stated his intention to serve the Lord. The New Testament continues the same theme. We've seen that in Romans 12:1 Paul called his readers to "present" themselves to the Lord "as a living sacrifice." The grammar of the verb *present* reveals that Paul expected them to reach a climactic *decision* of commitment leading to an ongoing *state* of commitment. The mercies of God, described in Romans 1–11, lead us all to a total commitment to God.

What are some of God's mercies that remind you of why you're totally committed to Him?

The good gifts that accompany salvation come to those who've completely committed themselves to God. Complete dedication also brings the resources needed for a life of holiness. As God showers His good gifts on us, He leads us in ways that will develop holiness. Then as we develop holy lives, God blesses us with a greater awareness of His presence.

CHOOSING HOLINESS DAY BY DAY. Day-by-day situations require decisions that reinforce and encourage the life of holiness within. Sometimes we're called to react in a Christlike way to unpleasant or difficult events. And at all times we have an ongoing responsibility to cultivate a lifestyle that reflects the glory of the holy God. Through both kinds of situations, God accomplishes His purpose of making us more Christlike.

Commands in Scripture, both direct and indirect, address our daily choices to be holy. The indirect commands come from logical applications of the teaching sections of the Bible. For example, Jesus told many parables that present God's truth in realistic situations, and every parable conveys at least an implied action. Jesus expected His hearers to understand the point of the parable and to act accordingly.

Similarly, passages dealing with the doctrine of Christ call for a response of worship and thanksgiving for what God has done through His Son (see Eph. 1:3-14; Col. 1:15-20; Heb. 1). These passages include implicit expectations that we honor Christ for who He is.

Read Colossians 1:15-20. What in this passage prompts you to worship?

Scripture also includes direct commands that encourage specific patterns of spiritual growth in the process of becoming holy. One example is found in Romans 6:

> Consider yourselves dead to sin but alive to God in Christ Jesus. Therefore do not let sin reign in your mortal body, so that you obey its desires.
>
> **ROMANS 6:11-12**

Two specific commands in this passage call for decisive action to overcome sin.

1. "Consider yourselves dead to sin but alive to God in Christ Jesus" (v. 11).

2. "Do not let sin reign in your mortal body, so that you obey its desires" (v. 12).

The second command is quite explicit in Greek. Literally, it says, "Stop letting sin reign in your mortal bodies." *Stop* implies the need for change from what characterizes life now to what life ought to be. Paul was equally clear in other passages addressing the old self and the new self. In Colossians 3:5 he said, "Put to death what belongs to your worldly nature." *Put to death* means *keep these things from expressing themselves as they did before conversion.* In verses 9 and 12 Paul used the image of changing clothes. He said, "You have taken off your old self" (v. 9, NIV). The metaphor is completed in verse 12, which says, "Clothe yourselves" (NIV) with the good qualities that accompany Christian living.

Read Colossians 3:5-15. What qualities did Paul tell believers to put to death?

What qualities did he tell believers to put on?

Paul often contrasted sinful conduct and righteous living in vice-and-virtue lists. The sinful list contains idolatry and immorality. These were sins the Jews identified as the primary indicators of pagan religion. Most pagan religious practices worshiped false gods and engaged in religious sexual orgies. Paul also included sins that represented a loss of control, such as anger or wrath, and social abuses. Finally, he often named sins of personal greed, such as covetousness.

By contrast, Paul instructed believers to clothe the new self with virtues that come from honoring the true God. They often included self-control, social respect, and fairness. Holiness means walking by the Spirit of God so that the old ways of living are replaced by the fruit of the Spirit (see Gal. 5:22-23).

These vices and virtues remind us of the necessity of volitionally cooperating with God by choosing holiness each day. Just as the Spirit of God doesn't override human personality and personal choices in bringing people to Christ, the Spirit of God won't violate human choices in life after conversion. While the Holy Spirit will urge believers toward holiness, as well as bring conviction about a wrong way of living, God won't force His way on us. However, He expects us to choose a new way of living based on new values and ambitions.

How can you be more intentional about making holy choices each day?

OPPOSITION TO GODLY CHOICES

Developing new patterns of life is never easy. God expects us to make the correct choices, but there's strong opposition to cultivating a life of holiness. This opposition comes from both outside and inside the believer.

EXTERNAL OPPOSITION. When we're converted, opposition to God's will intensifies. Knowledge is more difficult to obtain, proper choices more difficult to make, and new habits more difficult to practice because of spiritual warfare that arises around the new life in Christ. External opposition comes from the world, the flesh, and the Enemy.

The Bible repeatedly warns about pressures generated by the world. The Greek word for *world, cosmos,* literally means *the earth.* However, that's seldom its meaning in Scripture. Normally in Scripture the word *world* is a metaphor used to designate the world's systems. The world has a distinctive value system. It's a system of thought that's contrary to God and seeks to exclude God entirely.

Identify examples of world systems that are allied against God.

How do those systems lure believers away from holy choices?

John warned about the world's power:

> Do not love the world or the things that belong to the world.
> If anyone loves the world, love for the Father is not in him.
>
> **1 JOHN 2:15**

James issued a similar warning:

> Adulteresses! Don't you know that friendship with the
> world is hostility toward God? So whoever wants to
> be the world's friend becomes God's enemy.
>
> **JAMES 4:4**

These statements echo what both writers may have heard from Jesus Himself. Knowing His followers would be persecuted, He warned them to expect such conflict:

> If the world hates you, understand that it hated Me before
> it hated you. If you were of the world, the world would love
> you as its own. However, because you are not of the world,
> but I have chosen you out of it, the world hates you.
>
> **JOHN 15:18-19**

The world's systems and institutions keep us from God. Again John warned:

> The world with its lust is passing away, but the
> one who does God's will remains forever.
>
> **1 JOHN 2:17**

Our world doesn't promote holiness. Christians must make difficult, deliberate choices to separate themselves from the world and to become like Christ.

What are some ways believers can deliberately separate themselves from the world and choose God's ways?

The Bible also warns about the pressures of the flesh that work against a holy life. The Greek word for *flesh* means *the meat of a person or an animal.* Often in Scripture the word is used literally, but it also has a metaphorical meaning with moral connotations. The flesh is the natural way of thinking and acting, unaided by the Holy Spirit. The primary difference between the world and the flesh is that the world is an environment, a system constructed by people. The flesh is the natural way worldly people view life.

Like the world, the flesh is contrary to God. Paul warned about the dangers of following the flesh and about the personal and corporate destruction it causes.

Read Romans 8:5-8 and identify dangers of following the flesh.

Paul warned that thinking in the flesh brings death (see Rom. 8:6). It's preoccupied with wrong desires (see v. 5), "is hostile to God," and "cannot please God" (vv. 7-8).

Writing to the Galatian church, Paul named many works of the flesh:

> The works of the flesh are obvious: sexual immorality, moral impurity, promiscuity, idolatry, sorcery, hatreds, strife, jealousy, outbursts of anger, selfish ambitions, dissensions, factions, envy, drunkenness, carousing, and anything similar. I tell you about these things in advance—as I told you before—that those who practice such things will not inherit the kingdom of God.
>
> **GALATIANS 5:19-21**

The flesh is a characteristic way of viewing reality without considering God. It's the way unbelievers appraise things. Pressure from the flesh comes from the collective appraisals of all non-Christians, but it can also come from within a Christian. When Christians think and act like those without the Holy Spirit, they are living according to the flesh, as Paul once described the Corinthian church:

> I was not able to speak to you as spiritual people but as people of the flesh, as babies in Christ. I gave you milk to drink, not solid food, because you were not yet ready for it. In fact, you are still not ready, because you are still fleshly. For since there is envy and strife among you, are you not fleshly and living like unbelievers?
>
> **1 CORINTHIANS 3:1-3**

The task of becoming holy is to learn the way of the Spirit and to allow Him to overcome the way of the flesh.

> *Think about ways you're pressured to live in the flesh. Why do you think you have those tendencies?*

> *What are some ways believers can avoid living in the flesh?*

The Bible also describes pressures that come from the Enemy. The Bible refers to Satan in different ways, but all point to him as a slanderer, deceiver, and promoter of evil. The Devil opposes God and has done so from the beginning. John described him this way:

> The one who commits sin is of the Devil, for the Devil has sinned from the beginning. The Son of God was revealed for this purpose: to destroy the Devil's works.
>
> **1 JOHN 3:8**

Peter warned believers:

> Your adversary the Devil is prowling around like
> a roaring lion, looking for anyone he can devour.
>
> **1 PETER 5:8**

These warnings echo Jesus' explanation of Satan's activity. When Peter questioned Jesus, He responded:

> Get behind Me, Satan! You are an offense to Me because
> you're not thinking about God's concerns, but man's.
>
> **MATTHEW 16:23**

In accusing the Pharisees of colluding with the Devil, Jesus described him this way:

> You are of your father the Devil, and you want to carry out your father's
> desires. He was a murderer from the beginning and has not stood
> in the truth, because there is no truth in him. When he tells a lie, he
> speaks from his own nature, because he is a liar and the father of liars.
>
> **JOHN 8:44**

Satan opposes followers of Christ, seeking to blind their eyes so that they can't understand the truth. The Enemy seeks to counter the choices God's people should make.

> *Think of times and occasions when you're most susceptible to the Devil's influence. How can you stay alert to His deception and attacks so that you can choose holiness?*

External influences can make holy choices difficult. Some of the most pointed commands in Scripture warn about the world, the flesh, and the Devil. When believers take a strong stand for holiness and choose God's ways, they can expect opposition. Only by continually making holy choices can believers grow in the image of Christ.

INTERNAL OPPOSITION. Internal pressures also exert their influence on the Christian life. One task of believers is to possess a transformed mind that replaces the mind of the flesh with the mind of Christ. As Paul wrote, "We have the mind of Christ" (1 Cor. 2:16). The mind is progressively able to choose holiness when it progressively thinks in a holy way.

Other pressures war against the Christian's ability to make proper choices. These are described in Scripture as desires. In the Book of James we read:

> Each person is tempted when he is drawn away
> and enticed by his own evil desires.
>
> **JAMES 1:14**

Temptation has both inner and outer aspects. Outside there's a lure, something that attracts our attention. Inside we have desires or lusts that attract us to the outer lure. Temptation occurs in the interaction of these two.

Temptations fall into three major categories, although they manifest themselves in many specific ways.

1. One area of temptation is passion, represented by the phrases "good for food" (Gen. 3:6), "stones to become bread" (Matt. 4:3), and "lust of the flesh" (1 John 2:16). All people have difficulty learning to control their passions.

2. A second area of temptation is possessions, represented by the phrases "delightful to look at" (Gen. 3:6), "I will give You all these things" (Matt. 4:9), and "lust of the eyes" (1 John 2:16). People have a natural inclination to acquire things, and sometimes they acquire them in unethical, illegal, or unwise ways.

3. The final area of temptation is position, represented by the phrases "desirable for obtaining wisdom" (Gen. 3:6) and "pride in one's lifestyle" (1 John 2:16), as well as in the temptation for Jesus to throw Himself off the temple and summon angels to save Him. The drive to be something and to be seen as someone causes us to seek prominent positions in our own ways rather than doing the will of God.

The three types of temptation occur together in several passages and individually in many others. One of the composite passages is Genesis 3:6:

> The woman saw that the tree was good for food and delightful
> to look at, and that it was desirable for obtaining wisdom.
>
> **GENESIS 3:6**

Another passage is 1 John 2:16:

> Everything that belongs to the world—the lust of the
> flesh, the lust of the eyes, and the pride in one's lifestyle—
> is not from the Father, but is from the world.
>
> **1 JOHN 2:16**

And the final passage containing all three types of temptation is Matthew 4:1-11.

Read Matthew 4:1-11. What three ways did Satan tempt Jesus?

The specific temptation may vary, but we can be sure that the world, the flesh, and the Devil will take advantage of the desire to fulfill passions, acquire possessions, or occupy positions of power, leading us away from a life of holiness.

Describe a way a passion, possession, or position has diverted you from a course of holiness and spiritual growth.

Which is currently a greater obstacle in pursuing holiness—an external influence or an internal influence?

This discussion reveals the difficulty of making proper choices. It's not easy to choose what's right and what promotes a holy life. The naturally depraved mind, along with both external and internal opposition, means we must have a renewed mind and the resolve to choose correctly. Without proper choices there will be no growth toward holiness.

What's one way you can be more intentional about making holy choices?

POWER TO MAKE HOLY CHOICES

Perhaps the most crucial issue confronting those who want to live holy, changed lives is the ability to do it. Many times we know what's best and resolve to do it, but actually doing it is another matter. So what about people who can't seem to accomplish what they choose? The Bible promises help for all believers—the weak-willed as well as the mature. The Holy Spirit is accessible to help in times of difficulty and to empower our growth in Christlikeness. In fact, one of the Holy Spirit's tasks is to bring God's resources to us. He knows our weaknesses and our temptations, but He also knows the way to victory. The power for Christian living comes from the Holy Spirit.

The Holy Spirit brings actual liberation from sin and death. At conversion we die to sin with Christ. The Bible says we're "freed from sin's claims" (Rom. 6:7). *Justification* is a word that refers to a believer's standing with God. It points to the righteous legal status a believer has in Christ but doesn't address the experience of sinning. Because of our death with Christ, we're declared free from sin. However, being declared free isn't the same as experiencing freedom.

In Romans 8:2 a different word is used that literally means *liberation*. In that verse Paul explained that "the Spirit's law of life in Christ Jesus has set you free from the law of sin and of death." Here the word for *set free* is *liberates*. It means *enjoying the actual experience of freedom*. When we're set free, the Holy Spirit applies to us what Jesus accomplished on the cross and what we experienced at conversion.

> *How have you experienced the difficulty of living out the freedom you received through Christ?*

> *How have you experienced increasing freedom as you've followed Jesus awhile?*

Believers who seek to cooperate with the Holy Spirit's work desire the things of the Spirit (see Rom. 8:5-8). The Spirit works on the mind so that we value the new life in Christ. Our ambitions are what we desire, and the Holy Spirit enables us to desire the things of the Spirit. Thus, the Spirit works in the entire salvation experience. Paul explained:

You, however, are not in the flesh, but in the Spirit, since
the Spirit of God lives in you. But if anyone does not have
the Spirit of Christ, he does not belong to Him.

ROMANS 8:9

There's no need for a second experience in life to bring the presence of the Holy Spirit. He comes at conversion and immediately begins His work, urging the believer to higher things. This is why believers who sin experience a new kind of conviction. At conversion we become "wholeheartedly" obedient to God (Rom. 6:17, NIV). When we act out of harmony with our hearts, we experience frustration resulting from the conviction of the Holy Spirit.

There's much confusion about the sanctifying work of the Holy Spirit. Some teach the necessity of a Pentecostal experience to bring the sanctifying power of the Spirit. Nothing in Scripture confirms this position. No passage in Scripture suggests that a believer should seek an experience of any kind. In addition, the Spirit's presence at Pentecost had nothing to do with overcoming sin and achieving holiness.

Others refer to the Spirit's sanctifying work as the filling of the Spirit. Once again, there's confusion about that idea. Although there are Scripture passages in which the Greek words for *filling* occur in connection with the Holy Spirit, there's no passage that clearly associates the filling of the Spirit with holiness. As used in Luke and Acts, the Greek words for *filling* are never connected with holiness. Rather, they explain the ability to minister effectively. The words *filling* and *Holy Spirit* also occur together in Ephesians 5:18, but again, they have no connection to personal holiness.

In Galatians 5 Paul described the Holy Spirit's work in a believer.

Read Galatians 5:16-26. How does the Spirit help a believer live a holy life?

What are some characteristics of a life lived in the Spirit?

Paul used three verbs to describe the Spirit's presence in a Christian's life.

1. The first verb, *walk,* occurs in verse 16. The Greek is literally *walk around (peripateo).* A believer is to conduct all of life in the sphere of the Spirit.

2. The second verb, *led,* occurs in verse 18. If the Holy Spirit leads believers, they aren't under law. The Holy Spirit brings freedom from the law, giving internal standards rather than external ones and bringing God's power rather than self-effort.

3. The final verb is "keep in step with the Spirit" (v. 25, NIV); in Greek the word is *stoicheo.* This rare word means *to place our feet in the place the Spirit leads.* It was used of the military, which marched in step.

All these verbs contribute to a proper understanding of the Holy Spirit's role. We're to invite the Holy Spirit to be present in every aspect of life. We're to follow the Holy Spirit as He leads us. More precisely, we must do exactly what the Holy Spirit commands, putting our feet where the Spirit puts His. When believers do these things, they'll be characterized by the fruit of the Spirit (see vv. 22-23), not by the works of the flesh (see vv. 17,19-21).

To live a holy life and grow in Christlikeness, a believer must be primarily concerned with walking by the Spirit. The focus in Christian living is always obedience to Christ. The Holy Spirit empowers those who consistently follow Christ. Further, the more consistently we're growing in Christ and in doing the will of God, the more available the Spirit's resources are. As Christians focus on holy choices and on being obedient to God, the Holy Spirit's power comes to them. The Spirit renews the mind, applies the power of Christ, and leads in victory.

A learned skill in walking by the Spirit is discerning the balance between self-effort and appropriating God's power. Some people approach life assuming they must do everything by self-will. They treat God like a coach who stands on the sidelines and watches them play the game. Others approach life passively. Assuming Jesus will live through them, they exert no self-effort toward holiness. Usually, they're easily frustrated because they don't experience the victory they expect. If it's up to Jesus or the Spirit, why aren't they perfect immediately? Neither approach is biblical.

Which comes more easily in your Christian walk—self-effort or dependence on God to do everything? What have the results been?

Victory over sin comes in cooperation with the Holy Spirit. God generally doesn't do what we make no attempt to do. Part of correctly choosing to walk in holiness is exerting the effort to accomplish the choice made. On the other hand, even young Christians soon learn they can't handle spiritual battles in their own strength. Satan's power is simply too great. Without the Holy Spirit's help, there's no victory. A serious choice to be holy means a sincere effort to do God's will. At the same time, we must maintain a spirit of dependence and trust that the Holy Spirit will empower us to accomplish far more than we can on our own. Throughout Scripture God accomplished His work through human effort. The principle also applies to our efforts toward personal holiness.

The New Testament contrasts the Holy Spirit with the law. The Spirit brings supernatural power to a believer's life, while the law, with its emphasis on works, can only weaken us. The New Testament uniformly teaches that Christians no longer live under the law. The Gospels and the epistles warn us about living under the law. Writing to the church in Colosse, Paul affirmed:

> No one is justified by the works of the law but by faith in Jesus Christ. And we have believed in Christ Jesus so that we might be justified by faith in Christ and not by the works of the law, because by the works of the law no human being will be justified.
>
> **GALATIANS 2:16**

Christians are under grace, not law. Although the law has value in revealing God's character and expectations, it has no value in regulating the Christian life. The attempt to live by any law, including the Ten Commandments, brings frustration and impotence. The power the law seems to encourage is willpower. The law is external, imposing itself on us and calling for total obedience or else. The Jews of Paul's day believed their spiritual power resulted from keeping the law. But the only power they possessed was their own. In contrast, "if you are led by the Spirit, you are not under the law" (Gal. 5:18). The power the Spirit brings is God-power.

We all want to live powerful lives. If we want to have power, we must walk by the Holy Spirit. He freely brings God's power into our feeble lives, allowing us to accomplish everything God wills for us. Without the Holy Spirit we're left to our own strength and are hopeless. With God's powerful presence in our lives, we can triumph in His strength.

How have you experienced the Holy Spirit bringing power and victory to your desire to grow spiritually and to live a holy life?

Three essential ingredients promote growth. Without knowledge, proper choices, and the power of the Holy Spirit, Christians can't grow. All three efforts are necessary if Christians are to mature and be successful in the journey to holiness.

Assess your journey toward holiness by marking the scales.

1	2	3	4	5	6	7	8	9	10
Not growing in knowledge   *Growing in renewing my mind*

1	2	3	4	5	6	7	8	9	10
Choosing the world, flesh, and Devil   *Making holy choices*

1	2	3	4	5	6	7	8	9	10
Focused on self-effort   *Cooperating with the Spirit*

Spend time in prayer confessing areas of your life in which you're struggling to make choices that lead to Christlikeness. Ask God to help you form habits that move you toward spiritual transformation.

CHAPTER 5 GROUP EXPERIENCE
EFFECTING CHANGE

COMING TOGETHER

1. Would you describe yourself as holy? Why or why not?

2. Is the process of sanctification primarily your responsibility or God's? Explain.

KNOWLEDGE: THE MIND IN THE NEW TESTAMENT

1. Why is knowledge key in making changes in the Christian life?

2. Read the following verses.

Because they did not think it worthwhile to acknowledge God, God delivered them over to a worthless mind to do what is morally wrong.

ROMANS 1:28

The peace of God, which surpasses every thought,
will guard your hearts and minds in Christ Jesus.

PHILIPPIANS 4:7

Identify differences between an ungodly mind and a godly mind. How did God change your thinking after you became a believer?

3. The Bible says people without God have depraved minds. What beliefs and behaviors do you see today that result from depraved minds?

4. *Read the following verses.*

Brothers, by the mercies of God, I urge you to present your
bodies as a living sacrifice, holy and pleasing to God; this is
your spiritual worship. Do not be conformed to this age, but
be transformed by the renewing of your mind, so that you may
discern what is the good, pleasing, and perfect will of God.

ROMANS 12:1-2

*How do we present our bodies "as a living sacrifice" (v. 1)? How will this
bring about the renewal of the mind?*

5. *Why is it easy for believers to be conformed to the world?*

6. *What does it mean to "be transformed by the renewing of your mind" (v. 2)?*

KNOWLEDGE: CONTRASTING WAYS OF LIFE

1. *Read 1 Corinthians 6:9-11 and Galatians 5:19-24. What behaviors did Paul
identify as requiring a change of mind in order to become holy?*

2. *What are some qualities of a renewed mind?*

KNOWLEDGE: PRINCIPLES OF CHRISTIAN GROWTH

1. *Read the following verses.*

Consider yourselves dead to sin but alive to God in Christ
Jesus. Therefore do not let sin reign in your mortal body, so
that you obey its desires. And do not offer any parts of it to
sin as weapons for unrighteousness. But as those who are
alive from the dead, offer yourselves to God, and all the parts
of yourselves to God as weapons for righteousness.

ROMANS 6:11-13

What did Paul mean by "dead to sin but alive to God in Christ Jesus" (v. 11)?

2. How does considering yourself dead to sin but alive to God affect your thinking about living a holy life?

CHOICES: CHOICES PROMOTING HOLINESS

1. The author wrote, "We'll become what we choose to become." Do you agree or disagree? Why?

2. Have you ever experienced a time when you completely dedicated yourself to Christ in a separate commitment beyond your initial conversion? Share what that was like and why you felt it was necessary.

3. Read Colossians 3:5-15. What qualities did Paul command believers to put to death? To put on?

4. What kinds of day-to-day situations challenge believers to choose between sin and holiness?

CHOICES: OPPOSITION TO GODLY CHOICES

1. Read James 4:4.

Adulteresses! Don't you know that friendship with the world is hostility toward God? So whoever wants to be the world's friend becomes God's enemy.

How do the world's systems lure believers away from holy choices?

2. How can believers keep from being adversely influenced by the world?

3. Read Romans 8:5-8. Chapter 5 defined flesh as the natural way of thinking and acting, unaided by the Holy Spirit. How does the flesh lure believers away from holy choices?

4. How can believers avoid living in the flesh?

5. *Read Peter's warning about Satan.*

Your adversary the Devil is prowling around like
a roaring lion, looking for anyone he can devour.

1 PETER 5:8

How can the Devil lure believers away from holy choices?

6. *How can believers avoid the Devil's traps?*

7. *Read James 1:14.*

Each person is tempted when he is drawn away
and enticed by his own evil desires.

How can our own desires lure us away from holy choices?

8. *How does Jesus' response to temptation in Matthew 4 provide a model for us?*

POWER TO MAKE HOLY CHOICES

1. *How have you experienced difficulty in living out your freedom in Christ?
   Or conversely, how have you experienced the Holy Spirit helping you realize
   that freedom?*

2. *Read Galatians 5:16-26. What are some ways the Holy Spirit helps believers
   live holy lives? How did Paul say we're to cooperate with the Spirit's work
   in our lives?*

3. *What does it mean to walk by the Spirit?*

4. *How does the Spirit bring power and victory to our lives in ways the law can't?*

5. *Pray, thanking God for the Holy Spirit, who empowers you for holy living.
   Ask for His guidance in making holy choices each day.*

COMPLETE HOLINESS

REACHING THE GOAL

A dramatic event occurred during the 1992 Olympics. The four-hundred-meter race pitted in competition some of the best athletes in the world. A favorite was Derrick Redmond, a runner from Great Britain. Years of training, practice, mental preparation, and competition led him to this point in time. Like a finely tuned engine, he lined up for his greatest race. He made a good start and ran exactly as he'd planned. In the last turn he knew he had a chance.

Then the worst of his fears was realized. Beginning the stretch toward the finish line, he pulled a hamstring muscle and fell helplessly to the track. Derrick repeatedly tried to stand and finish the race but to no avail. No doubt his emotional pain was greater than the physical as he watched the remaining runners streak by and cross the finish line. But Derrick was a champion. Refusing to give up, he kept trying to walk and then crawl to the finish line. Knowing his chance for a medal was gone, he still struggled to finish the race.

One man in the crowd sensed the significance of the moment. He rushed to the rail, pushed away the guards, and ran to the hurting runner. The crowd's attention turned to the stranger. He knelt down, lifted the runner, and supported him as together they hobbled to the finish line. The crowd cheered for this great demonstration of spirit. Before Derrick crossed the finish line, the media researchers had identified the stranger from the crowd. It was Derrick's father.

This true story has many applications to our study of holiness. Christians run the race of their lives looking toward the finish line, when they'll see Christ. They know they'll finish, but sometimes the race brings unexpected circumstances. Because of the weaknesses of the flesh, we also know we need help. Everyone does. As Derrick's father rushed to the aid of his son, God provides the needed help for us to finish the course. Our Heavenly Father's enablement guarantees we'll finish.

Describe a time when you felt that you couldn't keep going.

Describe a time when God's intervention made all the difference.

In this chapter we'll discuss the helps God provides to keep us moving toward holiness. We'll also discuss the final stage of perfection. We've presented the definition of *holiness* and the way transformation occurs so that we can become progressively holy in this life. Now our thoughts turn to the future. Who's there to help, and what will the end of our transformational journey be?

HELPS FOR GROWING IN HOLINESS

The transformation from the old person's lifestyle to the new person's lifestyle requires resolve and commitment. Although the new life in Christ is the most rewarding life we can experience, living it can feel lonely and sometimes fearful. Success results when we take advantage of the tools God provides to help us grow in the likeness of His Son.

God communicates His nature, purposes, and will to us in two primary ways: natural, or general, revelation and special revelation.

NATURAL REVELATION

God reveals Himself through natural channels, including creation, human conscience and intellect, and history.

CREATION. Creation is God's handiwork. It demonstrates God's presence and greatness, much as a painting points to the quality of the painter.

Read Psalm 19:1-6. What does creation reveal about God?

In studying creation, we get a sense of order and power, good and evil, and the possibility of new life. However, knowledge gained about God through creation has serious limitations. Those who prefer to derive their theology only from nature will likely be misguided. Nature simply isn't clear enough.

HUMAN CONSCIENCE AND INTELLECT. God created us in His image. Even with our fall into sin and the resulting depravity, we all have a vestige of God's image in us. Paul spoke of this as the law of God "written on their hearts" (Rom. 2:15). As we live our lives, we discover universal moral laws. By studying human nature, we can arrive at some fairly accurate conclusions about what our Creator must be like. Based on our understanding of human characteristics and thought patterns, we can assume God is a God of love, justice, power, mercy, and personality. Because we're created in God's image, we can derive some knowledge of God from human reason. Even so, human reason alone will never construct an accurate picture of God. Left to ourselves, we'll never know how to live for Him.

HISTORY. God works in and through the affairs of life. God not only works through them but also orchestrates them in His own way:

> From one man He has made every nationality to live over the whole earth and has determined their appointed times and the boundaries of where they live. He did this so they might seek God, and perhaps they might reach out and find Him, though He is not far from each one of us.
>
> **ACTS 17:26-27**

A study of history should help us find God because He's always there. Yet history is too clouded with sin to derive a clear theology of God.

These examples of natural revelation help explain human ideas about God's expectations. But the conclusions can be seriously misguided because natural revelation is only a partial disclosure of God to people, whose minds are blinded to the truth by sin. Natural revelation is ultimately an inadequate aid to righteous living.

SPECIAL REVELATION

The Bible is by far the most important tool God has provided for us to grow in holiness. It's His most effective means of knowing Him and His ways. In inspiring the Bible, God devised a way to communicate His truth to us accurately and relevantly. He used human experience, observations, ideas, and situations as the vehicles through which He conveyed divine truth to people of all ages. The Bible supplements natural revelation, illuminating truths that can't be understood through nature.

What does the Bible teach that you can't learn from creation, human conscience, and history?

The Bible is our guide to growing in Christ and living holy lives. At the end of his life, the apostle Paul looked back over the years and ahead to the responsibilities Timothy would assume. Paul wrote:

> All Scripture is inspired by God and is profitable for teaching, for rebuking, for correcting, for training in righteousness, so that the man of God may be complete, equipped for every good work.
>
> **2 TIMOTHY 3:16-17**

A commitment to Christ and to holiness means a commitment to the Bible as the Word of God and the only sufficient guide for life and godliness. Christians throughout the centuries have found the more time they spend with the Bible, the better they live their lives. They've studied it seriously and meditated on it personally. God speaks through the words of Scripture, and the Holy Spirit uses them to provide spiritual stability and to develop Christian character. Yet the Bible isn't the end in itself. It bears witness to Jesus as Lord. It explains how we come to know Jesus, how we can be true to Him, and how we can grow to be more like Him.

PRAYER

Another crucial help in attaining a holy life is prayer. The example of Scripture and the testimonies of Christians through the centuries confirm that prayer is a means of grace by which God speaks directly to His children, hears their needs, and receives their praise. In prayer we develop our relationship with God, learn His expectations for our lives, and receive power and direction. Serious Christians devote themselves to prayer.

The Bible records many types of prayers. Some are for praise, expressing appreciation for who God is and what He's done (see Eph. 1:3-14). Other prayers consist of petition, bringing to God our concerns and expecting Him to understand and respond.

Christians prayed for help in times of political oppression (see Acts 4:23-31), guidance in understanding God's will (see Acts 10:9-23), and safety and deliverance (see Acts 12:5). Scripture also teaches us to pray for wisdom (see Jas. 1:5) and God's provision for our needs (see Matt. 6:9-13). We're to bathe all of life in prayer (see Phil. 4:6-7; Jas. 5:13-18).

We can specifically pray for holiness, knowing it's God's goal for our lives. Paul prayed for the holiness of the church at Ephesus:

> I pray also that the eyes of your heart may be enlightened
> in order that you may know the hope to which he has called
> you, the riches of his glorious inheritance in the saints, and
> his incomparably great power for us who believe.
>
> **EPHESIANS 1:18-19, NIV**

This prayer asks for the "eyes of your heart" to "be enlightened." This is a prayer for the illumination of the mind—knowledge—and of the heart—choices—so that God can reveal Himself. The goal of all holiness is to be like Christ. Holiness comes, in part, from an effective prayer life, and conversely, holiness promotes effective prayer.

What role has prayer played in your Christian growth?

CHRISTIAN COMMUNITY

Another aid in achieving holiness is Christian community. Christian community occurs through the church, a Christian's primary environment for spiritual growth. Believers who've attempted to grow in Christ without the church have encountered serious limitations. The church is the visible body of Christ. When people are placed in the spiritual body of Christ at conversion, they should immediately express that affiliation by becoming a part of the visible body of Christ through baptism and church membership. In the church Christians share their spiritual gifts, express mutual concerns and care for one another, and multiply their witness to the world around them. Christian community is essential for individual Christian growth in holiness.

What are specific ways your church is helping you grow in Christ?

In the Book of Ephesians, Paul highlighted the church's role in spiritual growth:

> He personally gave some to be apostles, some prophets, some
> evangelists, some pastors and teachers, for the training of the saints
> in the work of ministry, to build up the body of Christ, until we all
> reach unity in the faith and in the knowledge of God's Son, growing
> into a mature man with a stature measured by Christ's fullness.

EPHESIANS 4:11-13

What's the church's role in the spiritual growth of its members?

What's the goal of spiritual growth?

Christian leaders build up God's people for works of service. Service enables the church to grow in unity and knowledge. The final stage is "a stature measured by Christ's fullness" (v. 13). The various spiritual gifts build up the whole until each Christian arrives at the goal. As Christians grow together and honestly relate to one another, they "grow in every way into Him who is the head" (v. 15). Such growth is a group process with a clear goal for every believer to be like Christ.

There are other advantages to being part of a church. Using the body metaphor, Paul explained that every member has an important place in the fellowship (see 1 Cor. 12:14-26). When the church functions as it should, honor and loving concern are expressed for all. Everyone can grow to full maturity. There are always Christians who don't represent the body of Christ as we hope they would. Rather than scorning them, we should provide special care and nurture for them (see v. 23).

In addition, the church provides an environment to smooth out rough edges in believers' character and behavior. In community we care about our commitment to God and about our relationships with others in the church. That means both the individual and the group devote time and energy to heal one another. Christians should be sympathetic to others' weaknesses, as well as committed to the corporate growth of the church, so that all are encouraged to grow in the likeness of Christ.

Paul also explained that Christians can't understand the love of Christ as they should without other Christians. He described growth in love this way:

> I pray that you, being rooted and firmly established in love, may be able to comprehend with all the saints what is the length and width, height and depth of God's love, and to know the Messiah's love that surpasses knowledge, so you may be filled with all the fullness of God.
>
> **EPHESIANS 3:17-19**

Paul identified three stages in experiencing the love of Christ.

1. Christians are first "rooted and firmly established in love" (v. 17). The salvation experience is the greatest expression of God's love.

2. Christians should grow together in their understanding of love. As we see God's love expressed to and lived through others, we gain more insight into the magnificent breadth of God's love—"the length and width, height and depth" (v. 18).

3. As church members relate to one another, understanding and appreciating what God has done in one another, they come to know the fullness of His love.

   Describe a way you've seen your church's environment of love promote the spiritual growth of its members.

Individual Christians can't know everything by ourselves. Further, we can't grow into holiness by ourselves. Mutual relationships promote growth.

CHRISTIAN SERVICE

Ministry builds Christian character and holiness by causing us to search our motives, message, and methods of service. Spiritual work requires the power of the Holy Spirit. The Spirit works best through obedient people who are fully seeking to know Christ.

Regular service, therefore, causes us to examine our lives. Ministry takes us to the spiritual battleground where we war against powers stronger than human beings (see Eph. 6:10-18). Victory comes only from the power of Christ, and there's a correlation between victory in Christ and personal holiness.

Christians grow through service. If we desire to be holy, we must serve Christ.

If you're involved in ministry, how is it stimulating your growth in holiness?

SUFFERING

The final help in achieving holiness is suffering. On the surface this tool appears to be negative. No one chooses to suffer. Yet we know of scriptural and personal examples when God used suffering to bring Christians closer to Himself. God doesn't need suffering to accomplish His purposes, and He didn't ordain suffering. If we didn't live in a fallen world, there'd be no sickness, sorrow, or suffering. However, the Bible teaches that God works through human suffering. Whether it's physical, emotional, mental, relational, or spiritual suffering, God does something special in people who trust Him as they endure it.

Romans 5 describes a growth process beginning with trials, an externally induced cause of suffering:

> We know that affliction produces endurance, endurance produces proven character, and proven character produces hope. This hope will not disappoint us, because God's love has been poured out in our hearts through the Holy Spirit who was given to us.
>
> **ROMANS 5:3-5**

In this text character is the equivalent of holiness. It's a permanent quality in a believer. James reminded his readers of the same benefit:

> The testing of your faith produces endurance. But endurance must do its complete work, so that you may be mature and complete, lacking nothing.
>
> **JAMES 1:3-4**

How can suffering produce maturity in a believer?

Many consider trials to be periods of God's inactivity. Nothing could be further from the truth. These texts reveal that God is very positive and active during trials. God uses difficult times to move us toward holiness.

Trials also equip us to minister more effectively. Paul explained in 2 Corinthians 1:3-5 that God comforts His people so that they can comfort others with the same comfort He provides. God's comfort comes to us through the lens of Christ's suffering. Jesus Himself endured suffering that led to His death. The writer of Hebrews stated:

> In bringing many sons to glory, it was entirely appropriate that God—all things exist for Him and through Him—should make the source of their salvation perfect through sufferings.
>
> **HEBREWS 2:10**

Suffering promotes holiness, builds character, and results in effective ministry.

The suffering Jesus experienced enables Him to help others endure their suffering. Hebrews assures us:

> Since He Himself was tested and has suffered,
> He is able to help those who are tested.
>
> **HEBREWS 2:18**

Jesus' suffering gives Him sympathy for His followers who suffer. Further, Hebrews identifies preparation for ministry with suffering. Jesus learned obedience through suffering, and with obedience He accomplished His sacrificial death for us (see Heb. 5:7-9). Suffering and obedience uniquely prepare us for service to God.

In suffering we see God's remarkable grace. God uses situations that arise from a sinful environment to accomplish His purposes for a believer. Paul expressed the confidence we can have in God's good intentions for us, even in our suffering:

We know that all things work together for the good of those who love God: those who are called according to His purpose.

ROMANS 8:28

When Satan throws his best at us, God triumphs by using the situation to produce spiritual growth in the lives of His children.

Describe an experience of suffering that caused you to grow spiritually.

Mark the scales to indicate the degree to which you're taking advantage of the tools God has provided for your growth in holiness.

1	2	3	4	5	6	7	8	9	10
Ignoring general revelation   *Seeing God at work in the world*

1	2	3	4	5	6	7	8	9	10
Not reading the Bible   *Reading the Bible daily*

1	2	3	4	5	6	7	8	9	10
Neglecting prayer   *Praying continually*

1	2	3	4	5	6	7	8	9	10
No involvement in church   *Active involvement in church*

1	2	3	4	5	6	7	8	9	10
Not serving others   *Actively serving others*

1	2	3	4	5	6	7	8	9	10
Suffering in bitterness   *Looking to God in suffering*

THE COMPLETION OF HOLINESS

As we've seen, holiness may be divided into three stages:

1. Positional holiness   2. Progressive holiness   3. Perfect holiness

At conversion believers are made positionally holy, and at that stage comes a guarantee that holiness will be progressively completed in their lives. Finally when we arrive in heaven, we'll reach a state of complete holiness. Let's explore what that prospect means.

Sanctification and glorification overlap at certain points. Glorification is the biblical doctrine that describes the ultimate goal of believers' salvation. Our model is Jesus' return to heaven after His work of redemption on earth was completed. In His High Priestly prayer in John 17, Jesus prayed for His glorification:

> Father, glorify Me in Your presence
> with that glory I had with You
> before the world existed.
>
> **JOHN 17:5**

Jesus anxiously awaited the time when He'd be restored to His true glory. In Scripture His glorification is seen after the resurrection, when He appeared in a new state with a glorified body. Believers' hope is that we'll be glorified like Jesus.

THE GUARANTEE OF COMPLETE HOLINESS

The Bible clearly teaches that all who accept Christ will be like Him:

> We know that when He appears, we will be like
> Him because we will see Him as He is.
>
> **1 JOHN 3:2**

The guarantee of ultimate salvation and complete holiness doesn't depend on the believer. Just as God accepts sinners who trust in Christ, God perfects those who are in Christ. Many passages confirm this truth.

Our conformity to Christ was the purpose of our salvation. Paul described the entire process as God sees it:

> Those He foreknew He also predestined to be conformed to the image of His Son, so that He would be the firstborn among many brothers. And those He predestined, He also called; and those He called, He also justified; and those He justified, He also glorified.
>
> **ROMANS 8:29-30**

The two verses in this passage take two slightly different approaches to the same end. Verse 29 links foreknowledge and predestination. *Predestination* means *to draw the horizons of life in advance.* So God drew the boundaries of our lives as believers before we lived them. Every believer can expect to be like Christ. That's God's plan and His choice. *Complete holiness* means *being re-created in the image of Christ.* Verse 30 views the same end, using different words. There's an unbreakable chain of God's choices for us and His actions toward us. Once we're predestined, glorification is guaranteed.

What's your reaction to the fact that your glorification is guaranteed?

As proof of this guarantee, Paul explained that God gave us the Holy Spirit to assure us of future glory. In Ephesians 1 Paul used two metaphors for the Holy Spirit. The first occurs in verse 13:

> When you heard the message of truth, the gospel of your salvation, and when you believed in Him, you were also sealed with the promised Holy Spirit.
>
> **EPHESIANS 1:13**

In the first century a seal was a personalized guarantee of authenticity and protection. Frequently, it was used in the postal system of the day. When a person of influence posted a letter, the letter was sealed in wax. The process included melting hot wax on the flap of the letter. Then a personalized, engraved ring was pressed into the wax. The seal wouldn't be broken until the letter reached its recipient. Paul's use of the metaphor describes the Holy Spirit as God's seal on us. The seal guarantees we'll arrive at our intended destination.

The second metaphor, in Ephesians 1:14, comes from the economic practices of the day. Then, as now, someone would often purchase major items in stages—for example, a down payment to be followed by the complete price amount. Applying the terminology to Christians, Paul explained that the Holy Spirit is God's down payment:

> He is the down payment of our inheritance, for the
> redemption of the possession, to the praise of His glory.
>
> **EPHESIANS 1:14**

This verse indicates that God intends to complete the process He began. The Holy Spirit, who resides within believers, guarantees that God will bring us to glory.

Paul also associated our glorification with our identification with Jesus' death:

> If we have been joined with Him in the likeness of His death,
> we will certainly also be in the likeness of His resurrection.
>
> **ROMANS 6:5**

Christ's death means we'll share in the resurrection. Sin won't have final power over us. In fact, we'll be able to live someday without the limitations imposed by sin (see v. 14).

Scripture also associates the guarantee of glory with the love of Christ, best shown in His death. Paul wrote one of the most loved of all passages in this light:

> I am persuaded that not even death or life,
> angels or rulers,
> things present or things to come, hostile powers,
> height or depth, or any other created thing
> will have the power to separate us
> from the love of God that is in Christ Jesus our Lord!
>
> **ROMANS 8:38-39**

For what obstacles in your life would you like to claim the preceding verses?

Nothing can keep a believer from receiving every gift of holiness God planned.

MORAL PERFECTION

The most obvious aspect of complete holiness is moral perfection, a future state when we'll be able to live morally blameless lives in God's presence. Colossians 1:22 promises this for the believer:

> He has reconciled you by His [Christ's] physical body through His death, to present you holy, faultless, and blameless before Him.
>
> **COLOSSIANS 1:22**

Paul described holiness as faultless and blameless. *Faultless* means *perfect,* a picture of something created without flaw. *Blameless* means no one can indict us for any activity. No one can fault a believer for anything he or she has done. Together these terms speak powerfully to the concept of complete holiness. They take us to a future time when both our character and our activity will be completely holy. The process starts when God forgives our sins through Jesus' redeeming work. It continues as He works in our lives to transform us into the likeness of His Son.

Read Philippians 1:9-11 and identify changes that take place in a believer in the process toward moral perfection.

What evidence does your life show that you're being renewed in Christ's image?

Moral perfection will come when we have complete, full knowledge. Earlier we discussed the necessity of being transformed by having a renewed mind (see Rom. 12:2). As we've seen, knowledge is one essential aspect of personal growth. Paul taught that a time will come when believers will have complete knowledge and be completely transformed in Christ's image. He wrote:

> Now we see indistinctly, as in a mirror,
> but then face to face.
> Now I know in part,
> but then I will know fully,
> as I am fully known.
>
> **1 CORINTHIANS 13:12**

The apostle John expressed the same truth:

> We are God's children now, and what we will be has not
> yet been revealed. We know that when He appears, we
> will be like Him because we will see Him as He is.
>
> **1 JOHN 3:2**

The phrase "We will be like Him" refers to moral perfection, as Christ possessed. John used this idea to motivate his readers to purity, for in verse 3 he continued, "Everyone who has this hope in Him purifies himself, just as He is pure." Clearly, becoming like Christ brings purity, "just as He is pure."

Complete purity is our ultimate condition. Holiness was lost in the garden of Eden. The purpose of Jesus' death was to provide holiness for those who'd lost it, and God promises holiness to all who accept Christ. The moral perfection God intends will come, but it will come in the future. Complete sanctification will come at death, when we know fully, see Christ perfectly, and stand before Him without accusation. There's no sinless perfection in this life. In fact, John warned that those who believe they can achieve a condition of sinlessness are in error:

> If we say, "We have no sin," we are deceiving
> ourselves, and the truth is not in us.
>
> **1 JOHN 1:8**

Something beyond our ability must occur to change our hearts and bring us to a state of perfect holiness. One day God will bring us to perfection in His presence.

BODILY PERFECTION

There's a close connection between the body and the soul. We're shaped in large part by the attributes of our bodies. Much of how we think of ourselves and how we act toward others is a reaction to natural or physical characteristics. We can't conceive of ourselves without a body. The close connection between body and soul affects us spiritually. The vehicle through which temptations come is the body. The body allows us to visualize the object of temptation, and then the body acts to attain those temporary satisfactions. However, progressive holiness also occurs in the body.

Read the following verses and record what they teach about God's intention for the body's holiness.

Romans 6:12-13

Romans 12:1

1 Corinthians 6:13

These references indicate that the body is to become holy as well as the soul. Deeds done in the body have eternal significance because the body can be the vehicle for accomplishing God's will. As Paul said:

> We must all appear before the tribunal of Christ, so that each may be repaid for what he has done in the body, whether good or worthless.
>
> **2 CORINTHIANS 5:10**

God expects sanctification in the body. In a real sense, if it doesn't take place there, it won't take place. There's a deep theological reason for Scripture's admonitions about the body. It can be illustrated by the use of the body in sexual relationships. When God created us, He gave us the beauty and responsibility of reproduction. Immediately after creation God established the foundation for marriage, saying man and woman were to leave father and mother, cleave only to each other, and become one flesh (see Gen. 2:24).

From that point the Bible reveals God's plan that husband and wife are to be sexually faithful and monogamous. This is for human good, but Scripture also hints of a deeper reason. First Corinthians 6:13 warns about sexual immorality because the body is "for the Lord." According to 1 Corinthians 7:4, the body also belongs to the spouse, while on earth, in the relationship of marriage. However, in heaven there's no marriage or giving in marriage (see Matt. 22:30). Apparently, there will be no sexual relationships, since we'll be "like angels in heaven" (v. 30), who don't reproduce.

Why, then, does Scripture give so much emphasis to the purity of the body? The bodily resurrection is an important tenet of orthodox Christianity, and Paul argued at great length that the body will be resurrected (see 1 Cor. 15:35-58). God created our bodies. They belong to Him, and at conversion they become His dwelling place:

What agreement does God's sanctuary have with idols?
For we are the sanctuary of the living God, as God said:
    I will dwell among them
    and walk among them,
    and I will be their God,
    and they will be My people.

2 CORINTHIANS 6:16

At the resurrection our bodies will belong to God in a unique way. All this suggests that God has a special interest in our bodies. The transformation of the body is an important part of His plan for redemption. As sin inhabits our bodies on earth, redemption will reverse that, and our bodies will live without sin.

Sanctification can't be complete without including our bodies. The Bible states that God will transform our bodies so that they'll be perfect like the soul. Three primary passages from Paul's writings speak of this. In Philippians 3 Paul wrote:

Our citizenship is in heaven, from which we also eagerly wait for a Savior, the Lord Jesus Christ. He will transform the body of our humble condition into the likeness of His glorious body, by the power that enables Him to subject everything to Himself.

PHILIPPIANS 3:20-21

This text conveys two major truths about the perfection of the body.

1. The body will be transformed to be like Jesus' body. If we study the postresurrection passages in the Gospels, we learn that our heavenly bodies will be like Christ's body after His resurrection.

2. Jesus' power accomplishes the transformation of our bodies at the second coming. The completion of our holiness won't be achieved progressively. It will come climactically.

Paul further described the nature of the heavenly body.

Read the following passages and record details you find interesting about the nature of our heavenly bodies.

1 Corinthians 15:42-49

2 Corinthians 5:1-5

These passages show that our future bodies will be heavenly, not earthly, and therefore suited to heaven (see 2 Cor. 5:1-5). Because only perfection exists in heaven, the body will be perfect and perfectly suited to that environment. Further, it's a spiritually maintained body (see 1 Cor. 15:42-49), not flesh and blood, a feature suggesting that life in heaven is maintained by spiritual energy rather than air, food, and sun. Somehow spiritual power replaces the blood, so no longer is life in the blood as it is on earth (see Lev. 17:14).

While these passages teach us about the nature of the body, one verse explains the transformation that will take place:

> Just as we have borne the likeness of the earthly man,
> so shall we bear the likeness of the man from heaven.
>
> **1 CORINTHIANS 15:49, NIV**

"The likeness of the man from heaven" states the goal of being in the image of our Creator, the goal of holiness. The entire discussion of the eternal body relates to holiness. Without a transformation of the body, holiness is incomplete.

What are you most looking forward to about having a perfect resurrection body?

Although we long for perfection, we won't achieve it until death. At that time we'll have the moral perfection we seek. Similarly, our physical bodies long for complete redemption. We're restless of body just as we're restless of soul:

> We ourselves who have the Spirit as the firstfruits—
> we also groan within ourselves, eagerly waiting for
> adoption, the redemption of our bodies.
>
> **ROMANS 8:23**

Someday the body won't be the instrument of sin but of pure worship and service. Although our bodies on earth have limitations, someday these will be removed.

When God completes our redemption at the resurrection from the dead, we'll be whole. Holiness will become a reality. Both the material and the immaterial components of our being will be transformed into the image of Christ.

PRACTICAL IMPLICATIONS FOR LIVING A HOLY LIFE

No discussion of holiness is complete without a discussion of practical matters, because proper theology should always lead to balanced Christian living. Though many subjects in the previous chapters already lend themselves to practical applications, the following ideas may help you organize and implement the truths you've learned.

HOLINESS COMES FROM KNOWING OUR DESTINATION. God saved us to shape us into the restored image of Christ, and He will accomplish that in us. Knowing that provides direction in life. Every Christian should intentionally seek to grow in Christ and to live a holy life that honors Him. As we've seen, the Bible gives a clear picture of a holy life on earth, leading to complete holiness in heaven. We should meditate on what we'll be, then seek day by day to live holy lives in accordance with our decision to follow Christ.

HOLINESS COMES FROM MAKING GODLY CHOICES. Greater knowledge brings greater responsibility, but it doesn't necessarily bring a better way of life. Wishing to live in the manner we know is best begins a process, but wishing alone doesn't help. In fact, many people live in frustration because they don't achieve their spiritual desires. The commands in God's Word call for a response. The emphasis in Scripture is on continually choosing a holy way of life. Scripture affirms that spiritual transformation comes through personal choices. Although everyone needs God's power to effect radical change in life, the direct commands of the Bible teach that the individual can and must choose to live for God.

HOLINESS COMES FROM DISCIPLINED OBEDIENCE. People err when they assume a mystical experience will suddenly make them holy. Scripture doesn't support that idea. Another mistake is to hope God will do the work of holiness for us, but passive people don't just arrive at holiness. And then there's the idea that we don't need to exercise discipline to achieve holiness. Christians testify that the single most important secret to growing in holiness is to walk with Christ in an intentional, disciplined way. Regular times of Bible study, prayer, worship, and ministry bring multiplied benefits over time. God's power comes to those who obey Christ and allow Him to mold their lives in His image.

HOLINESS COMES FROM SETTING THE RIGHT GOAL. Many Christians measure their holiness by how far they've come since conversion. Certainly, looking back encourages us when we observe how much our lives have changed. People often rejoice as they look back over their shoulders and view the distance between them and the non-Christian world. But a Christian's goal is to be like Christ, not merely to be different from the world. Separation is never the ultimate goal; Christlikeness is. Using any other benchmark for success causes us to measure ourselves by external, temporal reference points that foster pride and divide Christians from one another.

Consider the previous implications and identify one or more adjustments you'll make to grow in holiness.

A study like this forces us to fall on our faces in humility and confession, knowing we don't measure up to the righteous standards of our Lord Jesus Christ. But we can always grow in our Christian lives. In the days ahead may we be found faithful to our high and holy calling. We must live every day fully trusting in God's love, forgiveness, strength, and purposes for us. We're new people, and we have new power and new potential. May we develop to our full potential in Christ.

Finally, we should have strong confidence that God will complete what He started. The moment of conversion we were assured of complete victory. Our confidence is that God will guide us to glory, where we'll fellowship with Him in a completely holy state. Our confidence in His good work brings hope day by day. Even if life seems overwhelming and the world, the flesh, and the Enemy seem overwhelming, God will give us victory. Holiness is becoming like Jesus Christ day by day, step by step, relationship by relationship, and victory by victory. We are victors, not victims, because we know:

> He who started a good work in you will carry it
> on to completion until the day of Christ Jesus.
>
> **PHILIPPIANS 1:6**

May our Lord make it so!

Thank God for His plan to redeem you, transform you to be like Jesus, and bring you to complete holiness. Tell Him your desire to live a holy life and any changes you need to make. Ask Him to empower and enable your growth.

CHAPTER 6 GROUP EXPERIENCE
REACHING THE GOAL

COMING TOGETHER

1. How can the Christian life be compared to a race?

2. What help do you need to finish the race of life?

HELPS FOR GROWING IN HOLINESS: NATURAL REVELATION

1. How do the following means of natural revelation contribute to our growth in holiness?

- *Creation*

- *Human conscience and intellect*

- *History*

2. Is natural revelation all we need to become holy? Why or why not?

HELPS FOR GROWING IN HOLINESS: SPECIAL REVELATION

1. Read the following verses.

All Scripture is inspired by God and is profitable for teaching, for rebuking, for correcting, for training in righteousness, so that the man of God may be complete, equipped for every good work.

2 TIMOTHY 3:16-17

What guidance does the Bible provide for our sanctification?

2. Share ways the Bible has personally helped you grow in Christlikeness.

HELPS FOR GROWING IN HOLINESS: PRAYER

1. Read the following verses.

I pray also that the eyes of your heart may be enlightened
in order that you may know the hope to which he has called
you, the riches of his glorious inheritance in the saints, and
his incomparably great power for us who believe.

EPHESIANS 1:18-19, NIV

How do Paul's requests specifically relate to a holy walk with God?

2. How can prayer help believers grow in Christ?

HELPS FOR GROWING IN HOLINESS: CHRISTIAN COMMUNITY

1. Read the following verses.

He personally gave some to be apostles, some prophets, some
evangelists, some pastors and teachers, for the training of the saints
in the work of ministry, to build up the body of Christ, until we all
reach unity in the faith and in the knowledge of God's Son, growing
into a mature man with a stature measured by Christ's fullness.

EPHESIANS 4:11-13

What is the goal of spiritual growth?

2. What is the church's role in developing its members' spiritual growth?

3. In what ways is your church fulfilling that role?

HELPS FOR GROWING IN HOLINESS: CHRISTIAN SERVICE

1. How does Christian service encourage us to grow in holiness?

*2. How have you grown or seen others grow in maturity through
Christian service?*

HELPS FOR GROWING IN HOLINESS: SUFFERING

1. Read Romans 5:3-5. How does God use our suffering to bring spiritual growth in our lives?

2. Read Romans 8:28.

We know that all things work together for the good of those who love God: those who are called according to His purpose.

Identify the requirements to see God work for your good in suffering.

THE COMPLETION OF HOLINESS: THE GUARANTEE

1. Read Romans 8:29-30.

Those He foreknew He also predestined to be conformed to the image of His Son, so that He would be the firstborn among many brothers. And those He predestined, He also called; and those He called, He also justified; and those He justified, He also glorified.

Who's responsible for justifying, sanctifying, and glorifying believers?

2. Read the following verses.

When you heard the message of truth, the gospel of your salvation, and when you believed in Him, you were also sealed with the promised Holy Spirit. He is the down payment of our inheritance, for the redemption of the possession, to the praise of His glory.

EPHESIANS 1:13-14

What does it mean for the Holy Spirit to be the seal and down payment of our inheritance?

3. Describe your feelings when you think about being glorified in God's presence.

THE COMPLETION OF HOLINESS:
MORAL AND BODILY PERFECTION

1. Read Colossians 1:22.

He has reconciled you by His physical body through His death,
to present you holy, faultless, and blameless before Him.

What qualities do you associate with moral perfection?

2. What's your response to the prospect of being morally perfect when you get to heaven?

3. Read Philippians 3:20-21. What's your response to the prospect of having a new body in heaven?

PRACTICAL IMPLICATIONS FOR LIVING A HOLY LIFE

1. Discuss how each of the following suggestions can help you live a more holy life.

• Know your destination.

• Make godly choices.

• Practice disciplined obedience.

• Set the right goal.

2. Share any commitments you'll make to pursue a more holy life and more diligent growth in the likeness of Jesus.

3. End the study by thanking God for the provision He's made for you to grow in the likeness of Jesus and to be glorifed in His presence someday. Ask Him to enable you to actively pursue holiness, at the same time relying on and cooperating with Him to bring to completion His work of sanctification and glorification in your life.